DICTATORSHIP, FASCISM, AND TOTALITARIANISM

DICTATORSHIP, FASCISM, AND TOTALITARIANISM

Edited by Shalini Saxena

Britannica®
Educational Publishing

IN ASSOCIATION WITH

ROSEN
EDUCATIONAL SERVICES

Published in 2015 by Britannica Educational Publishing (a trademark of Encyclopædia Britannica, Inc.) in association with The Rosen Publishing Group, Inc. 29 East 21st Street, New York, NY 10010

Distributed exclusively by Rosen Publishing.
To see additional Britannica Educational Publishing titles, go to rosenpublishing.com.

First Edition

Britannica Educational Publishing
J.E. Luebering: Director, Core Reference Group
Anthony L. Green: Editor, Compton's by Britannica

Rosen Publishing
Hope Lourie Killcoyne: Executive Editor
Shalini Saxena: Editor
Nelson Sá: Art Director
Nicole Russo: Designer
Cindy Reiman: Photography Manager
Karen Huang: Photo Researcher
Introduction and supplementary material by Jacob Steinberg

Cataloging-in-Publication Data

Dictatorship, fascism, and totalitarianism/edited by Shalini Saxena.—First Edition.
    pages cm.—(Political and economic systems)
Includes bibliographical references and index.
ISBN 978-1-62275-350-5 (library bound)
1. Dictatorship—Juvenile literature. 2. Fascism—Juvenile literature. 3. Totalitarianism—Juvenile literature. I. Saxena, Shalini, 1982–
JC495 .D4827
321.9—dc23

2014004691

Manufactured in the United States of America

On the cover, p. 3: © *iStockphoto.com/bjones27*

CONTENTS

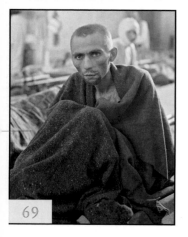

87

102

116

INTRODUCTION

In a speech given at a National Socialist German Workers' Party convention in Augsburg, Germany, on July 6, 1923, future chancellor of Germany Adolf Hitler summarized a key principle of what would soon become one of history's most infamous authoritarian governments. He stated, "Majority resolutions of a parliament cannot save us; only the value of a unique personality can do that. As *Führer* [dictator] of the National Socialist Party, I see my task as assuming full responsibility. We do not rely upon committees and majorities... National Socialists demand from their leader that he renounce all vanity and expressions of personal admiration; he must not worry about what the majority of people want him to do, but must carry out whatever his conscience before God and man tells him is necessary."

Hitler's fiery speech at that convention was telling of the type of authoritarian government he would soon come to establish across Germany and much of north-central Europe. In political theory, authoritarianism denotes any political system that concentrates power in the hands of a leader or a small elite that is not constitutionally responsible to the body of the people. While many authoritarian leaders initially rise to power through constitutional means, their power often comes to exceed the established legal limits of their positions and presents a serious challenge to the free will of their citizens.

At the turn of the 20th century, the global political and economic situation seemed assuredly stable. The preeminence of diplomacy and alliances among the powerful nations of Europe meant that by 1914, just under a decade before Hitler's fervent Augsburg speech, the continent had seen forty-three years of peace, and most nations had focused

Adolf Hitler with members of the SA, the German paramilitary organization that helped him rise to power. Hitler established a totalitarian dictatorship based on fascist ideals. Imagno/Hulton Archive/Getty Images

their efforts on either domestic matters or the maintenance of vast overseas holdings in the form of colonies, if not a balance of both.

As the world progressed into the 20th century, however, political history was increasingly shaped by the changing relations of the world's great powers. The first half of the century—the age of the World Wars and the start of the Cold War—was dominated by a break in diplomacy and the rivalries of those powers. The second half saw the replacement, largely through the agency of those wars, of the European state system by a world system with many centres of both power and discord. The effects of World War I politicized economic relations within and between countries, and the needs of internal stability conflicted with the needs of international stability. Old dreams clashed with new realities, and new dreams with old realities.

As people sought new political systems to accommodate these new realities, a sharp contrast was drawn between two types of government that came to dominate modern political states: "autocratic" and "nonautocratic" governments. Totalitarianism is only a recent species of autocracy, to which constitutionalism is the principal contemporary antithesis.

Autocracy is characterized by the concentration of power in a single centre, be it an individual dictator or a group of power holders such as a committee or party leadership. This centre relies on force to suppress opposition and to limit social developments that might eventuate in opposition. The power of the centre is not subject to effective controls or limited by genuine sanctions: it is absolute power.

In appearance, autocracy may sometimes be difficult to distinguish from nonautocratic rule. Often, autocracies attempt to borrow legitimacy by adopting the language of the constitutions of nonautocratic regimes or by establishing similar institutions.

It is a common practice, for example, in many modern totalitarian states to establish institutions—parliaments or assemblies, elections and parties, courts and legal codes—that differ little in appearance from the institutional structures of constitutional democracies. Similarly, the language of totalitarian constitutions is often couched in terms of the doctrines of popular rule or democracy.

The fundamental difference is that in totalitarian regimes neither the institutions nor the constitutional provisions act as effective checks on the power of the single centre: they are essentially facades for the exercise of power through hierarchical procedures that subject all the officials of the state to the commands of the ruling individual or group. The underlying realities of autocratic rule are always the concentration of power in a single centre and the mobilization of force to prevent the emergence of opposition.

Across the political spectrum there are several related, yet distinct, manifestations of an autocratic form of government. Modern dictatorships have a close, albeit complicated relationship with other monocracies or authoritarian forms of government such as totalitarianism, and with such ideologies as fascism. Totalitarianism may be seen as the most extreme form of an authoritarian government in which the state widely controls most aspects of society and mobilizes citizens and social life toward a singular goal. In fascist states this societal control and the ultimate goal toward which they purport to work is blended with nationalistic policies or racist attitudes as well.

Authoritarian leaders often exercise power arbitrarily and without regard to existing bodies of law, and they usually cannot be replaced by citizens choosing freely among various competitors in elections. The freedom to create opposition political parties or other alternative political groupings with which to compete for power with the ruling group is either limited or nonexistent in authoritarian regimes.

Dictatorship is a form of authoritarianism in which the government rules without the consent of those being governed—in direct contrast to democracy. Totalitarianism, in turn, is another form of authoritarianism in which the state regulates every aspect of social life and public behavior of its citizens, often mobilizing them toward a common state goal—in contrast to the principle of pluralism. Fascist governments often specifically use totalitarian means to promote national unity or identity, invoking the primacy of the state above all other rights or freedoms.

While royal rule, as legitimized by blood descent, had almost vanished as an effective principle of government in the modern world, monocracy—a term that comprehends the rule of non-Western royal absolutists, of generals and strongmen in Latin America and Asia, of a number of leaders in postcolonial Africa, and of the totalitarian heads of communist states—still flourished. Indeed, the 20th century, which witnessed the careers of Kemal Atatürk, Benito Mussolini, Adolf Hitler, Joseph Stalin, Francisco Franco, Mao Zedong, Juan Perón, Josip Broz Tito, Gamal Abdel Nasser, Sukarno, Kwame Nkrumah, and Charles de Gaulle, could go down in history as the age of plebiscitary dictatorship.

Although similar in some respects to the dictatorships of the new countries, the *caudillos* of 19th- and 20th-century Latin America represented a very different type of monocratic rule. In its 19th-century form, *caudillismo* was the result of the breakdown of central authority. After a brief period of constitutional rule, each of the former Spanish colonies in the Americas experienced a collapse of effective national government. A self-proclaimed leader, usually an army officer, heading a private army typically formed from the peasantry with the support of provincial landowners, established his control over one or more provinces and then marched upon the national capital. The famous 19th-century caudillos—Antonio López de Santa Anna of Mexico or Juan Manuel de Rosas of Argentina, for example—were thus essentially provincial leaders who seized control of the national government to maintain the social and economic power of provincial groups. The 20th-century dictatorships in Latin American countries had different aims.

The modern caudillo proved to be less a provincial leader than a national one. The Perón regime, for example, was established by nationalistic army officers committed to a program of national reform and ideological goals. Often, too, 20th-century dictators in Latin America allied themselves with a particular social class, attempting either to maintain the interests of established economic groupings or to press social reforms.

Dictatorship in the technologically advanced, totalitarian regimes of modern communism was distinctively different from the authoritarian regimes of either Latin America or the postcolonial states of Africa and Asia. Totalitarianism, as already noted, has been a chief form of autocratic rule; it is distinguished from previous forms in its use of state power to impose an official ideology on its citizens. Nonconformity of opinion is treated as the equivalent of resistance or opposition to the government, and a formidable apparatus of compulsion, including various kinds of state police or secret police, is maintained to enforce the orthodoxy of the proclaimed doctrines of the state. A single party, centrally directed and composed exclusively of loyal supporters of the regime, is the other typical feature of totalitarianism. The party is at once an instrument of social control, a vehicle for ideological indoctrination, and the body from which the ruling group recruits its members.

Nazi Germany under Hitler and the Soviet Union under Stalin are the leading examples of modern totalitarian dictatorships. Most of the sub-Saharan African nations are also one-party dictatorships, and other examples can be found in the Middle East and Latin America. South Africa presented an unusual situation. For its white citizens it was a constitutional democracy, but for its more than 22 million blacks it was a dictatorship that bordered upon totalitarian control.

What distinguishes a traditional dictatorship—particularly the 20th-century variety—from totalitarianism is primarily the extent of control. Dictatorships are usually satisfied to control the political apparatus of a country. This control is maintained through an extensive police network or through the army. The functions of the police or army are to maintain peace and to root out opposition. But as long as the government can operate without opposition, the rest of society's institutions are left to themselves if they do not set themselves up against the dictator.

In a totalitarian government all previous political institutions and constitutions are swept away and replaced by new ones. In the case of Nazi Germany and the Stalinist Soviet Union, the traditional institutions were replaced by individuals: Hitler and Stalin, respectively. They were the constitution, the law, and the government embodied in one person.

In addition to political domination, everything else and everyone is put into the service of the country. The government manages and operates the economy and monitors all production and consumption. All writers and artists, if they are to hold jobs, must belong to the government-operated union. All scientific research is done for the government. Schools serve the goals of the government in their classwork in addition to teaching regular subject matter. Drama, opera, ballet, and athletics are controlled and supported by the government. Religion, if not outlawed altogether, is closely watched by the government, which also takes over some of its functions.

Western constitutional democracies have provided examples of another type of contemporary dictatorship. Throughout the 20th and 21st centuries, most constitutional regimes have granted the executive emergency powers during periods of domestic or foreign crisis. Constitutional guarantees of individual rights or liberties are not guaranteed or some form of martial law is declared. The U.S. Constitution provides limited emergency power, allowing for the suspension of ordinary judicial process in the event of war, invasion, or rebellion, but this authority is granted to Congress rather than to the president. Constitutions of some other Western democracies have similar provisions.

This practice was particularly essential in the constitution of Weimar Germany, which came into effect after World War I. The emergency provisions in the Weimar constitution were invoked more than 200 times, initially to combat violent insurrection and direct threats to the maintenance of the constitutional system itself. In the early 1930s, however, these provisions were invoked with increasing frequency to combat a wide range of social and domestic problems, including economic failure. Although these provisions probably allowed Weimar Germany to survive, ultimately, these provisions also allowed Adolf Hitler to seize and consolidate his power, formally exercising the constitution's emergency powers as chancellor in 1933. There are many other instances of dictators using such provisions to overthrow a regime: Mussolini in Italy, Atatürk in Turkey, Józef Piłsudski in Poland, António de Olveira Salazar in Portugal, Franz von Papen in Germany, and Engelbert Dollfuss and Kurt von Schuschnigg in Austria. Despite such examples, however, many democracies have withstood long periods of crisis government. Emergency powers debates are not limited to the West, of course, and have been particularly relevant in Eastern Europe, Africa, Latin America, and South Asia, where newly consolidating democracies struggled with challenges to their survival and with the abuse of delegated power, notably in India in 1971, Russia in the 1990s, and in the former Yugoslavia.

In the pages that follow, the history of authoritarian governments will be assessed. Whether dictatorships employed by constitutional means, or fascist coups d'état seeking to impose conservative traditions and nationalistic ideologies, autocratic thought has had a huge impact on political thought, influencing policy in both authoritarian states and their democratic counterparts.

CHAPTER 1

DICTATORSHIP

A dictatorship is a form of government in which one person or a small group possesses absolute power without effective constitutional limitations. The term *dictatorship* comes from the Latin title *dictator*, which in the Roman Republic designated a temporary magistrate who was granted extraordinary powers in order to deal with state crises. Modern dictators, however, resemble ancient tyrants rather than ancient dictators. Ancient philosophers' descriptions of the tyrannies of Greece and Sicily go far toward characterizing modern dictatorships. Dictators usually resort to force or fraud to gain despotic political power, which they maintain through the use of intimidation, terror, and the suppression of basic civil liberties. They may also employ techniques of mass propaganda in order to sustain their public support.

Tyrants and Dictators in Ancient Times

A tyrant was a cruel and oppressive ruler or, in ancient Greece, a ruler who seized power unconstitutionally or inherited such power. In the 10th and 9th centuries BCE, monarchy had been the usual form of government in the Greek states; the aristocratic regimes that had replaced monarchy were by the 7th century BCE themselves unpopular. Thus the opportunity arose for ambitious men to seize power in the name of the oppressed.

The best-known tyrannies were those founded by Cypselus at Corinth and Orthagoras at Sicyon about 650 BCE. There were tyrants also in Asiatic Greece, the most famous of whom was Thrasybulus of Miletus (c. 600). The tyrants often sprang from the fringe of the aristocracy; for example, the mother of Cypselus belonged to the ruling clan of the Bacchiads, but his father did not. The nature of the public discontent that provided them with a following may have varied from place to place. At Sicyon, Cleisthenes, who ruled from about 600 to about 570 and was the most successful of the Orthagorids, expressed or exploited the resentment felt by the non-Dorian and underprivileged element in society toward those who claimed descent from the Dorian invaders. Some historians have supposed that the introduction of the hoplite phalanx early in the 7th century led to the development of a class of substantial farmers, who served in the phalanx and supported the tyrants as their champions against the aristocracies. But although the tyrants may have made use of hoplite tactics, substantial farmers were probably a conservative, not a revolutionary, force, and there is no reason to suppose that farmer-hoplites developed class consciousness.

Tyrants eventually came to be considered oppressive, especially by their rivals for political power. Cypselus's son Periander, whose powerful reign at Corinth lasted about 40 years, came to be regarded as a typically bad tyrant. The Corinthian tyranny fell in the late 580s soon after he died.

Sparta, which had developed a constitution under which all citizens were soldiers and theoretically equal, avoided tyranny. Peisistratus established a tyranny at Athens in the middle of the 6th century; his son Hippias was expelled by King Cleomenes I of Sparta in 510. This may be taken as the end of the "age of tyrants" but not the end of tyranny. The

Periander, marble bust; in the Vatican Museums, Vatican City. The Mansell
Collection/Art Resource, New York

Persians preferred to keep tyrants in charge of the Greek cities of Anatolia, which they conquered about 540.

In the west, where military autocracy easily took root, the popularity of Gelon of Syracuse rested to a great extent on his defeat of the Carthaginians at Himera in 480; his brother and successor, Hieron, patron of Pindar and others, won a celebrated victory over the Etruscans at Cumae in 474. In 405 Dionysius I of Syracuse, the most powerful of all tyrants, first established his rule during the crisis of another Carthaginian invasion.

In the Hellenistic period some tyrants rested their power on class feeling; others were foreign nominees, like the tyrants supported by the Macedonian kings in the Peloponnese in the 3rd century. The phenomenon continued as long as Greece was free. The great tyrants were notable patrons of the arts and conspicuous builders. They often aided in the transition from narrow aristocracy to more democratic constitutions, but the Greeks in principle chafed under their illegal autocracy; thus tyranny early acquired a bad name, and tyrannicides such as Harmodius and Aristogiton, who killed Hippias's brother Hipparchus at Athens, received the highest honours.

In contrast to a tyrant, in the Roman Republic, a dictator was a temporary magistrate with extraordinary powers, nominated by a consul on the recommendation of the Senate and confirmed by the Comitia Curiata (a popular assembly). The dictatorship was a permanent office among some of the Latin states of Italy, but at Rome it was resorted to only in times of military, and later internal, crises. The dictator's term was set at six months, although he customarily laid down his powers as soon as the crisis passed. He had 24 *fasces*, the equivalent of both consuls. His first act was to appoint as his immediate subordinate a master of the cavalry (*magister equitum*). The consuls and other magistrates continued in office during a dictatorship but were subject to the dictator's authority. By the 3rd century BCE the limited term of a dictatorship rendered it impracticable in operations outside of Italy. Moreover, by 300 BCE the people had secured the limitation of dictatorial powers by subjecting their use to the right of appeal and to a tribune's veto. Dictators were then named for lesser functions such as the holding of elections in certain cases.

The Carthaginian invasion in the Second Punic War (218–201 BCE) spurred a temporary revival of the office, but after 202 no dictators were chosen for any purpose. The dictatorships conferred upon Sulla and Julius Caesar in the last decades of the republic, in the 1st century BCE, did not indicate a revival of the former office but the development of an extraconstitutional office with virtually unlimited powers. Sulla's and Caesar's dictatorships were not for a limited emergency but rather were meant "to restore the republic," a reason mentioned as legitimate in Cicero's *De republica* (54– 52; *On the Republic*). The term of office was lengthened until Caesar acquired dictatorial powers for 10 years in 46 and for life immediately before his assassination in 44 BCE, when the office was abolished.

The Dictatorship of Julius Caesar

In Rome the administrative machine had inevitably been disrupted following the civil war of 49–45 BCE, and Julius Caesar had always remained in control, as consul or as dictator. Those who had feared proscriptions, or hoped for them, were proved wrong. Some of Caesar's enemies had their property confiscated, but it was sold at fair value; most were pardoned and suffered no loss. Poverty and indebtedness were alleviated,

(continued on the next page)

but there was no wholesale cancellation of debts or redistribution of property, and many of Caesar's adherents were disappointed. Nor was there a general reform of the republic. (Caesar's only major reform was of the calendar: indeed, the Julian calendar proved adequate for centuries.) The number of senators and magistrates was increased, the citizenship was more freely given, and the province of Asia was relieved of some of its tax burden. But Caesar had no plan for reforming the system—not even to the extent that Sulla had tried to do, for Sulla had at least planned for his own retirement.

For a time, honourable men, such as Cicero, hoped that the "Dictator for Settling the Constitution" (as Caesar called himself) would produce a real constitution—some return to free institutions. By late 45 that hope was dead. Caesar was everywhere, doing everything to an almost superhuman

Julius Caesar, leading the first Roman invasion of Britain in 55 BCE. Universal Images Group/SuperStock

degree. He had no solution for the crisis of the republic except to embody it in himself and none at all for the hatred of his peers, which he knew this was causing. He began to accept more and more of the honours that a subservient Senate invidiously offered, until finally he reached a position perilously close to kingship (an accursed term in Rome) and even deification. Whether he passed those hazy boundary lines is much debated and not very important. He had put himself in a position in which no Roman ought to have been and which no Roman aristocrat could tolerate. As a loyal friend of his was later to say: "With all his genius, he saw no way out." To escape the problem or postpone it, he prepared for a Parthian war to avenge Crassus—a project most likely to have ended in similar disaster. Before he could start on it, about 60 men—former friends and old enemies, honourable patriots and men with grievances—struck him down in the Senate on March 15, 44 BCE.

Dictatorship Through the Early 19th Century

Following the dictatorships of Lucius Cornelius Sulla and Julius Caesar, as well as the negative connotations that the title "dictator" came to acquire under these leaders, the Roman office of dictatorship was abolished in 44 BCE. With the transition from the Roman Republic into the Roman Empire, the Latin title *imperator* ("emperor") was regularly adopted by rulers as a forename and gradually came to apply to the office that these rulers occupied. Thus, the title of dictator went out of style until its reemergence several hundred years later.

The Reign of Terror

Following the establishment of the Roman office of emperor, the term *dictator* would not make a prominent reappearance in political history until the time of the French Revolution. The French Revolution was a revolutionary movement that shook France between 1787 and 1799 and reached its first climax there in 1789.

Initially, the National Constituent Assembly—a revolutionary assembly formed by deputies of the Third Estate (the commoners) that subsequently came to include the nobles and clergymen as well—tried to create a monarchical regime in which the legislative and executive powers were shared between the king and an assembly. This regime might have worked if the king had really wanted to govern with the new authorities, but Louis XVI was weak and vacillating and was the prisoner of his aristocratic advisers. On June 20–21, 1791, he tried to flee the country, but he was stopped at Varennes and brought back to Paris.

By early 1792 both radicals, eager to spread the principles of the Revolution, and the king, hopeful that war would either strengthen his authority or allow foreign armies to rescue him, supported an aggressive foreign policy. France declared war against Austria on April 20, 1792.

In the first phase of the war (April–September 1792), France suffered defeats; Prussia joined the war in July, and an Austro-Prussian army crossed the frontier and advanced rapidly toward Paris. Believing that they had been betrayed by the king and the aristocrats, the Paris revolutionaries rose on August 10, 1792, occupied Tuileries Palace, where Louis XVI was living, and imprisoned the royal family in the Temple.

With the meeting of the National Convention on September 21, 1792, came the establishment of the First French Republic, as well as the trial and execution of former king Louis XVI.

As the war continued and the flailing French economy also fed civil unrest, the Convention was bitterly divided almost to the point of paralysis. From the opening day, two outspoken groups of deputies vied for the support of their less factional colleagues. These two opposing groups were known as the Girondins and the Montagnards. After significant debates and a variety of political tactics, by the end of May 1793 a majority seemed ready to support the Montagnards. The Girondins were swiftly expelled by eager Parisian militants. The ongoing events of the French Revolution, coupled with the political instability of the National Convention, laid the groundwork for the assumption of what effectively became a dictatorship by assemblyman Maximilien de Robespierre.

After the fall of the Girondins, the Montagnards were left to deal with the country's desperate position. Threatened from within by the movement for federalism and by the civil war in the Vendée in the northwest and threatened at the frontiers by the anti-French coalition, the Revolution mobilized its resources for victory. In his diary, Robespierre noted that what was needed was *"une volonté une"* ("one single will"), and this dictatorial power was to characterize the Revolutionary government. Its essential organs had been created, and he set himself to make them work.

On July 27, 1793, Robespierre took his place on the Committee of Public Safety, which had first been set up in April. While some of his colleagues were away on missions and others were preoccupied with special assignments, he strove to prevent division among the revolutionaries by relying on the political group known as the Jacobin societies, as well as the vigilance committees. Henceforward his actions were to be inseparable from those of the government as a whole. As president of the Jacobin Club and then of the National Convention, he denounced the schemes of the Parisian radicals known as the Enragés, who were using the food shortage to stir up the Paris sections. Robespierre answered the demonstrators on

September 5 by promising maximum prices for all foodstuffs and a Revolutionary militia for use in the interior against counterrevolutionaries and grain hoarders.

In order to bring about a mass conscription, economic dictatorship, and total war, he asked to intensify the Reign of Terror. But he objected to pointless executions, protecting those deputies who had protested the arrest of the Girondins and of the king's sister. He was sickened by the massacres condoned by the *représentants en mission* (members of the National Convention sent to break the opposition in the provinces) and demanded their recall for "dishonouring the Revolution."

Robespierre devoted his report of 5 Nivôse, year II (December 25, 1793 [the French republican calendar had been introduced in September 1793, with its beginning, or year I, set one year prior]), to justifying the collective dictatorship of the National Convention, administrative centralization, and the purging of local authorities. He protested against the various factions that threatened the government. The Hébertists, the Cordeliers, and the popular militants all called for more-radical measures and encouraged de-Christianization and the prosecution of food hoarders. Their excesses frightened the peasants, who could not have been pleased by the decrees of 8 and 13 Ventôse, year II (February 26 and March 3, 1794), which provided for the distribution among the poor of the property of suspects.

Reappearing at the Jacobin Club after a month's illness, Robespierre denounced the radical revolutionist Jacques-René Hébert and his adherents, who together with some foreign agents were executed in March. Those who wanted, like Georges Danton, to halt the Reign of Terror and the war attacked the policies of the Committee of Public Safety with increasing violence. Robespierre, although still hesitant, led the National Convention against these so-called Indulgents. The Dantonist leaders and the deputies who were compromised in the liquidation of the French East India Company were guillotined on 16 Germinal (April 5).

A deist in the style of Rousseau, Robespierre disapproved of the anti-Christian movement and the "masquerades" of the cult of reason. In a report to the National Convention in May, he affirmed the existence of God and the immortality of the soul and strove to rally the revolutionaries around a civic religion and the cult of the Supreme Being. That he remained extremely popular is shown by the public ovations he received after Henri Admirat's unsuccessful attempt on his life on 3 Prairial (May 22). The National Convention elected him president, on 16 Prairial (June 4), by a vote of 216 out of 220. In this capacity he led the festival of the Supreme Being ("Etre suprême") in the Tuileries Gardens on 20 Prairial (June 8), which was to provide his enemies with another weapon against him.

After the law of 22 Prairial (June 10) reorganizing the Revolutionary Tribunal, which had been formed in March 1793 to condemn all enemies of the regime, opposition to Robespierre grew; it was led by those *représentants en mission* whom he had threatened. By that time the Jacobin dictatorship had forged an effective government and had mobilized the nation's resources, thereby mastering the crisis that had brought it into being. Yet, on 8 Thermidor (July 26), Robespierre took the rostrum to proclaim his own probity and to denounce yet another unnamed group as traitors hatching "a conspiracy against liberty." Robespierre had clearly lost his grip on reality in his obsession with national unity and virtue. An awkward coalition of moderates, Jacobin pragmatists, rival deputies, and extremists who rightly felt threatened by the "Incorruptible" (as he was known) finally combined to

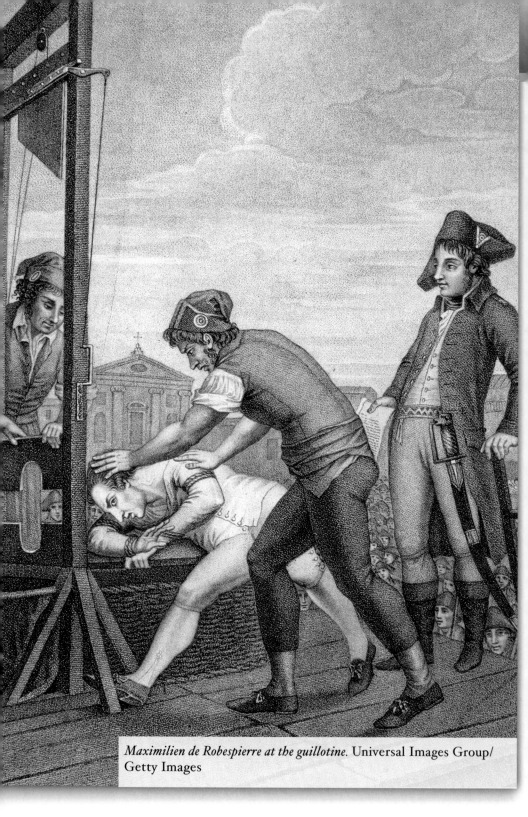

Maximilien de Robespierre at the guillotine. Universal Images Group/ Getty Images

topple Robespierre and his closest followers. On 9 Thermidor, year II (July 27, 1794), the Convention ordered the arrest of Robespierre and Saint-Just, and, after a failed resistance by loyalists in the Paris Commune, they were guillotined without trial the following day. The Terror was over, and power was distributed between a five-person "Directory" and a two-chamber legislative branch.

The Rise of Napoleon

The Directory, French *Directoire*, was set up by the Constitution of the Year III, and lasted four years, from November 1795 to November 1799. In hindsight, the Directory was a fatal experiment in weak executive powers; it was created in reaction to the puritanical dictatorship that had existed under the Reign of Terror of 1793–94, and it would end up yielding to the more disciplined dictatorship of Napoleon Bonaparte.

    The Directory suffered from widespread corruption. Its policies aimed at protecting the positions of those who had supported the Revolution and preventing the return of the Bourbons. Despite its unsavory reputation, it consolidated many of the achievements of the National Convention, such as the creation of a system of elite centralized schools, the *grandes écoles*. The French economy recovered from the disruption caused by the Terror, and the successes of the French armies laid the basis for the conquests of the Napoleonic period.

    A series of coups d'état were ultimately responsible for the ultimate disbandment of the Directory, chiefly those of 18 Fructidor, year V (September 4, 1797), which removed the royalists from the Directory and from the councils, and of 18 Brumaire, year VIII (November 9, 1799), in which Bonaparte abolished the Directory and became the leader of France as its "first consul."

Ahead of the coup d'état that would consolidate his dictatorial power, Napoleon Bonaparte had grown in prestige as a commander in the French army, carrying out successful campaigns across Europe and the Near East.

Bonaparte's return to Paris and coup led to the establishment of the Consulate, a three-member consul consisting of Bonaparte and two of the directors who had resigned from the Directory, Emmanuel Sieyès and Pierre-Roger Ducos. But it was Bonaparte who was henceforth the master of France.

As leader of France, Bonaparte showed himself to be a man of the 18th century, the most enlightened of the enlightened despots, a true son of Voltaire. He did not believe in the sovereignty of the people, in the popular will, or in parliamentary debate. Yet he put his confidence more in reasoning than in reason and may be said to have preferred "men of talent"—mathematicians, jurists, and statesmen, for instance, however cynical or mercenary they might be—to "technicians" in the true sense of the word. He believed that an enlightened and firm will could do anything if it had the support of bayonets; he despised and feared the masses; and, as for public opinion, he considered that he could mold and direct it as he pleased. He has been called the most "civilian" of generals, but essentially he never ceased to be a soldier.

Bonaparte imposed a dictatorship on France, but its true character was at first disguised by the constitution of the year VIII (4 Nivôse, year VIII; December 25, 1799), drawn up by Sieyès. This constitution did not guarantee the "rights of man" or make any mention of "liberty, equality, and fraternity," but it did reassure the partisans of the Revolution by proclaiming the irrevocability of the sale of national property and by upholding the legislation against the émigrés. It gave immense powers to the first consul, leaving only a nominal role to his two colleagues. The first consul—namely,

Bonaparte—was to appoint ministers, generals, civil servants, magistrates, and the members of the Council of State and even was to have an overwhelming influence in the choice of members for the three legislative assemblies, though their members were theoretically to be chosen by universal suffrage. Submitted to a plebiscite, the constitution won by an overwhelming majority in February 1800.

Facing the risk of royalist insurgencies encouraged by foreign enemies, Bonaparte was convinced that the best way to discourage conspiracy would be to transform the life consulate into a hereditary empire, which, because of the fact that there would be an heir, would remove all hope of changing the regime by assassination. Bonaparte readily accepted the suggestion, and on May 28, 1804, the

Detail of the Coronation of Napoleon in Notre-Dame *by Jacques-Louis David.* Peter Barritt/SuperStock/Getty Images

empire was proclaimed. Through popular reforms and a series of decisive military victories, Bonaparte consolidated his empire.

It was not until 1812 that the French Empire demonstrated signs of weakness. In fall and winter of that year, the Bonaparte-led French army faced disaster in Russia and was forced to retreat. News of the failure cause anti-French tides to sweep over Europe and encouraged a nearly successful coup back in Paris, only thwarted by Napoleon's return from war. Arriving in Paris on December 18, he proceeded to stiffen the dictatorship, to raise money by various expedients, and to levy new troops.

Nonetheless, foreign concerns over Bonaparte's dictatorial power and bellicose nature gave way to the Treaty of Chaumont of March 1814, in which Austria, Russia, Prussia, and Great Britain bound themselves together for 20 years, undertook not to negotiate separately, and promised to continue the struggle until Napoleon was overthrown. When the allied armies arrived before Paris on March 30, Napoleon had moved east to attack their rear guard. The Parisian authorities, no longer overawed by the emperor, lost no time in treating with the allies. As president of the provisional government, Talleyrand proclaimed the deposition of the emperor and, without consulting the French people, began to negotiate with Louis XVIII, the brother of the executed Louis XVI. Napoleon had only reached Fontainebleau when he heard that Paris had capitulated. Persuaded that further resistance was useless, he finally abdicated on April 6.

Napoleon first faced exile on the Mediterranean island of Elba, where the allies allowed him to keep the nominal title of "emperor" and a personal guard of four hundred men. He later returned and briefly returned to power in France, only to find himself exiled again—this time in the British-controlled South Atlantic island of St. Helena.

Decline of the Hereditary Monarchy

When he crowned himself Emperor of France in 1804 (and ratified the act by a people's referendum), Napoleon Bonaparte instituted a new type of monarchy. This was the "nationalist monarchy," whereby the monarch ruled on behalf of his society's nationalist aspirations and drive for independence (as opposed to the earlier types of legitimacy). Napoleon based his rule on the instruments of the French Revolution, such as the Declaration of the Rights of Man and of the Citizen.

The outcome of the French Revolution and developments in political thought throughout the 19th century would ultimately lead to a decline in monarchies based on hereditary descent as the dominant political institution. This decline, in turn, would pave the ground for the re-emergence of dictatorships in many countries, although in a decidedly different sense than the dictators of ancient Rome.

Dictators in the 19th and 20th Centuries

With the decline and disappearance in the 19th and 20th centuries of monarchies based on hereditary descent, dictatorship became one of the two chief forms of government in use by nations throughout the world, the other being constitutional democracy. Rule by dictators has taken several different forms. In some instances, self-proclaimed leaders tried to establish control over a territory with their armies before marching upon a weak national government. In other instances, leaders were put in their position of power by nationalistic military officers. Other dictators came to power by election, after which they captured personal power by establishing one-party rule and suppressing the opposition. In addition, sometimes an army or group of army officers seized power and established a military dictatorship.

Latin America

In Latin America in the 19th century, various dictators arose after effective central authority had collapsed in the new nations recently freed from Spanish colonial rule. These *caudillos*, or self-proclaimed leaders, usually led a private army and tried to establish control over a territory before marching upon a weak national government. Antonio López de Santa Anna in Mexico and Juan Manuel de Rosas in Argentina are examples of such leaders. Later 20th-century dictators in Latin America were different. They were national rather than provincial leaders and often were put in their position of power by nationalistic military officers, as was Juan Perón of Argentina. They usually allied themselves with a particular social class, and attempted either to maintain the interests of wealthy and privileged elites or to institute far-reaching left-wing social reforms.In Latin America, *personalismo* denoted the practice of glorifying a single leader, with the resulting subordination of the interests of political parties and ideologies and of constitutional government.

Latin American political parties have often been constituted by the personal following of a leader rather than by adherents of certain political beliefs or proponents of certain issues. Thus the popular term for such parties or their members has been often derived from their leaders—e.g., Peronistas (the followers of Juan Perón, Argentine president in 1946–55, 1973–74) or Fidelistas (the followers of Fidel Castro,

Cuban leader who came to power in 1959). The archetypical demagogue and focus of *personalismo* in Mexico was General Antonio López de Santa Anna, who dominated Mexican political life between 1821 and 1855. The Dominican Republic and Ecuador in particular have suffered from *personalismo*, but the phenomenon has been rather pervasive throughout Latin American history.

Personalismo is related to the phenomenon in Latin America called *caudillismo*, by which a government is controlled by leaders whose power typically rests on some combination of force and personal charisma (*caudillos*). During and immediately after the Latin American independence movement in the early 19th century, politically unstable conditions led to the widespread emergence of such leaders; thus the period is often referred to as the "age of the *caudillos*." The flamboyant leader of the independence movement, Simón Bolívar, was one such ruler (of Gran Colombia, his ephemeral political creation). Although some nations, such as Argentina and Chile, developed more regular forms of constitutional government in the latter 19th century, *caudillismo* remained into the 20th century a common feature of Latin American states and prevailed in such countries as Argentina, during Perón's regime—as a form of political bossism—and in others as outright and brutal military dictatorship, as with the regime of Juan Vicente Gómez in Venezuela (ruled 1908–35). The latter was a ruler in the Venezuelan tradition, following the pattern of such strongmen as José Antonio Páez, who controlled the country in 1830–46 and again in 1860–63. Among other well-known *caudillos* of the 19th century were Juan Manuel de Rosas of Argentina, Francisco Solano López of Paraguay, and Andrés Santa Cruz of Bolivia. In such countries as Argentina and Mexico, during periods of weak central government, regional *caudillos* operated in their own localities in much the same way as did those on a national scale.

Juan Perón

Juan Domingo Perón (b. Oct. 8, 1895, Lobos, Buenos Aires *provincia*, Argentina–d. July 1, 1974, Buenos Aires) in his career was in many ways typical of the upwardly mobile, lower-middle-class youth of Argentina. He entered military school at 16 and made somewhat better than average progress through the officer ranks. A strongly built six-foot-tall youth, Perón became the champion fencer of the army and a fine skier and boxer. He served in Chile as a military attaché and travelled to Italy to observe the rise of the Fascists and Nazis during 1938–40. He had a bent for history and political philosophy and published in those fields.

Perón returned to Argentina in 1941, used his acquired knowledge to achieve the rank of colonel, and joined the United Officers Group (Grupo de Oficiales Unidos; GOU), a secret military lodge that engineered the 1943 coup that overthrew the ineffective civilian government of Argentina. The military regimes of the following three years came increasingly under the influence of Perón, who had shrewdly requested for himself only the minor post of secretary of labour and social welfare. In 1944, however, as a protégé of Pres. Gen. Edelmiro J. Farrell (1944–46), Perón became minister of war and then vice president. Clearly he was bidding for undisputed power, based on the support of the underprivileged labourers (the *descamisados*, or "shirtless ones") and on his popularity and authority in the army.

In early October 1945, Perón was ousted from his positions by a coup of rival army and navy officers. But associates in the labour unions rallied the workers of greater Buenos Aires, and Perón was released from custody on Oct. 17, 1945. That night, from the balcony of the presidential palace, he addressed 300,000 people, and his address was broadcast to the country on radio. He promised to lead the people to victory in the pending presidential election and to build with them a strong and just nation. A few days later he married actress

Juan and Eva Perón riding through a street in Buenos Aires, Argentina. Rolls Press/Popperfoto/Getty Images

Eva Duarte, or Evita, as she became popularly called, who would help him rule Argentina in the years ahead.

After a campaign marked by repression of the liberal opposition by the federal police and by strong-arm squads, Perón was elected president in February 1946 with 56 percent of the popular vote.

Perón set Argentina on a course of industrialization and state intervention in the economy, calculated to provide greater economic and social benefits for the working class. He also adopted a strong anti-United States and anti-British position, preaching the virtues of his so-called *justicialismo* ("social justice") and "Third Position," an authoritarian and populist system between communism and capitalism.

(continued on the next page)

If Perón did not structurally revolutionize Argentina, he did reshape the country, bringing needed benefits to industrial workers in the form of wage increases and fringe benefits. He nationalized the railroads and other utilities and financed public works on a large scale. The funds for those costly innovations—and for the graft that early began to corrode his regime—came from the foreign exchange accumulated by Argentine exports during World War II and from the profits of the state agency that set the prices for agricultural products. Perón dictated the political life of the country by his command of the armed forces. He severely restricted and in some areas eliminated constitutional liberties, and in 1949 he arranged a convention to write a new constitution that would permit his reelection.

Reelected leader of the Justicialist Party (Partido Justicialista) by a somewhat larger margin in 1951, Perón modified some of his policies. But he was overthrown and fled to Paraguay on Sept. 19, 1955, after an army-navy revolt led by democratically inspired officers who reflected growing popular discontent with inflation, corruption, demagoguery, and oppression.

Perón finally settled in Madrid. There in 1961 he married for the third time (his first wife had died of cancer, as had Evita in 1952); his new wife was the former María Estela (called Isabel) Martínez, an Argentine dancer. In Spain, Perón worked to ensure, if not his return to Argentina, at least the eventual assumption of power by the millions of Peronist followers, whose memory of his regime improved with time and with the incapacity of the Argentine governments following Perón's decade of power.

In election after election the Peronists emerged as a large, indigestible mass in the Argentine body politic. Neither the civilian nor the military regimes that precariously ruled in Argentina after 1955 were able to solve the relatively rich country's condition of "dynamic stagnation," in part because they refused to give political office to the Peronists.

The military regime of Gen. Alejandro Lanusse, which took power in March 1971, proclaimed its intention to restore constitutional democracy by the end of 1973 and allowed the reestablishment of political parties, including the Peronist party. Upon invitation from the military government, Perón returned to Argentina for a short time in November 1972. In the elections of March 1973, Peronist candidates captured the presidency and majorities in the legislature, and, in June, Perón was welcomed back to Argentina with wild excitement. In October, in a special election, he was elected president and, at his insistence, his wife—whom the Argentines disliked and resented—became vice president.

While in exile Perón had wooed the left-wing Peronists and had supported the most belligerent labour unions. Once returned to power, however, he formed close links with the armed forces and other previously opposition right-wing groups. When he died in 1974, he left to his widow and successor as president an untenable situation. Isabel Perón failed to obtain the firm support of any power group, not even the labour unions. Terrorist activity and political violence increased. On March 24, 1976, the armed forces took power, removed Isabel Perón from office, and set up a military junta.

Africa and Asia

In the new states of Africa and Asia after World War II, dictators quickly established themselves on the ruins of constitutional arrangements inherited from the Western colonial powers that had proved unworkable in the absence of a strong middle class and in the face of local traditions of autocratic rule. In some such countries, elected presidents and prime ministers captured personal power by establishing one-party rule and suppressing the opposition, while in others the army seized power and established military dictatorships.

Whether as presidential dictatorships or as military dictatorships, the regimes that came into being appear to have had common roots in the social and economic problems of the new state. The constitutional systems inherited from the colonial powers proved unworkable in the absence of a strong middle class; local traditions of autocratic rule retained a powerful influence; the army, one of the few organized forces in society, was also often the only force capable of maintaining order; and a tiny intellectual class was impatient for economic progress, frustrated by the lack of opportunity, and deeply influenced by the example of authoritarianism in other countries. The dictatorships that resulted proved highly unstable, and few of the individual dictators were able to satisfy for long the demands of the different groups that supported their bids for power.

Western Europe and the Soviet Union

The communist and fascist dictatorships that arose in various technologically advanced countries in the first half of the 20th century were distinctively different from the authoritarian regimes of Latin America or the postcolonial dictatorships of Africa and Asia. Nazi Germany under Adolf Hitler and the Soviet Union under Joseph Stalin were the leading examples of such modern totalitarian dictatorships. The crucial elements of both were the identification of the state with a single mass party and of the party with its charismatic leader, the use of an official ideology to legitimize and maintain the regime, the use of terror and propaganda to suppress dissent and stifle opposition, and the use of modern science and technology to control the economy and individual behaviour. Soviet-type communist dictatorships arose in Central and Eastern Europe, China, and other countries in the wake of World War II, though most of them (as well as the Soviet Union itself) had collapsed by the last decade of the 20th century. The two systems, however, may be distinguished in several ways. Fascism, in its National Socialist form, was primarily a counterrevolutionary movement that mobilized middle- and lower-middle-class groups to pursue nationalistic and militaristic goals and whose sole principle of organization was obedience to the Führer. By contrast, Soviet communism grew out of a revolutionary theory of society, pursued the goal of revolutionary overthrow of capitalist systems internationally, and employed the complex bureaucratic structures of the Communist Party as mechanisms of governmental organization.

During times of domestic or foreign crisis, even most constitutional governments have conferred emergency powers on the chief executive, and in some notable cases this provided the opportunity for duly elected leaders to overthrow democracy and rule dictatorially thereafter. The proclamation of emergency rule, for example, was the beginning

António de Oliveira Salazar (left) *walking amongst Portuguese troops in 1940.* Keystone-France/Gamma-Keystone/Getty Images

of the dictatorships of Hitler in Germany, Benito Mussolini in Italy, Kemal Atatürk in Turkey, Józef Piłsudski in Poland, and António de Oliveira Salazar in Portugal. In other democracies, however, constitutional arrangements have survived quite lengthy periods of crisis, as in Great Britain and the United States during World War II, in which the use of extraordinary powers by the executive came to a halt with the end of the wartime emergency. Similarly, although the 1958 constitution of the Fifth Republic of France contained far-reaching emergency powers conferred on the president—"when the institutions of the Republic, the independence of the nation, the integrity of its territory or the fulfillment of its international obligations are threatened with immediate and grave danger, and when the regular functioning of the constitutional authority is interrupted"—their implicit threat to the constitutional order has not been realized.

Many forces at work in the late 20th and early 21st centuries have appeared to lend impetus to the rise of monocratic forms of rule. In nearly all political systems, the powers of chief executives have increased in response to the demanding social, economic, and military crises of the age. The complex decisions required of governments in a technological era, the perfectionist impulses of the great bureaucratic structures that have developed in all industrialized societies, and the imperatives of national survival in a nuclear world continue to add to the process of executive aggrandizement. The question for many constitutional regimes is whether the limitation and balance of power that are at the heart of constitutional government can survive the growing enlargement of executive power.

CHAPTER 2

COMMON CHARACTERISTICS OF FASCIST MOVEMENTS

Fascism is a political ideology and mass movement that dominated many parts of Central, Southern, and Eastern Europe between 1919 and 1945 and that also had adherents in Western Europe, the United States, South Africa, Japan, Latin America, and the Middle East. Europe's first fascist leader, Benito Mussolini, took the name of his party from the Latin word *fasces*, which referred to a bundle of elm or birch rods (usually containing an ax) used as a symbol of penal authority in ancient Rome.

Although fascist parties and movements differed significantly from each other, they had many characteristics in common, including extreme militaristic nationalism, contempt for electoral democracy

Fasces, a bundle of rods with an axhead, symbolized penal authority in ancient Rome and later became the emblem of the Italian Fascist Party as well as the inspiration for its name. Leemage/Universal Images Group/Getty Images

and political and cultural liberalism, a belief in natural social hierarchy and the rule of elites, and the desire to create a *Volksgemeinschaft* (German: "people's community"), in which individual interests would be subordinated to the good of the nation. At the end of World War II, the major European fascist parties were broken up, and in some countries (such as Italy and West Germany) they were officially banned. Beginning in the late 1940s, however, many fascist-oriented parties and movements were founded in Europe as well as in Latin America and South Africa. Although some European "neofascist" groups attracted large followings, especially in Italy and France, none were as influential as the major fascist parties of the interwar period.

There has been considerable disagreement among historians and political scientists about the nature of fascism. Some scholars, for example, regard it as a socially radical movement with ideological ties to the Jacobins of the French Revolution, whereas others see it as an extreme form of conservatism inspired by a 19th-century backlash against the ideals of the Enlightenment. Some find fascism deeply irrational, whereas others are impressed with the rationality with which it served the material interests of its supporters. Similarly, some attempt to explain fascist demonologies as the expression of irrationally misdirected anger and frustration, whereas others emphasize the rational ways in which these demonologies were used to perpetuate professional or class advantages. Finally, whereas some consider fascism to be motivated primarily by its aspirations—by a desire for cultural "regeneration" and the creation of a "new man"—others place greater weight on fascism's "anxieties"—on its fear of communist revolution and even of left-centrist electoral victories.

One reason for these disagreements is that the two historical regimes that are today regarded as paradigmatically fascist—Mussolini's Italy and Nazi Germany—were different in important respects. In Italy, for example, anti-Semitism was officially rejected before 1934, and it was not until 1938 that Mussolini enacted a series of anti-Semitic measures in order to solidify his new military alliance with Hitler. Another reason is the fascists' well-known opportunism— i.e., their willingness to make changes in official party positions in order to win elections or consolidate power. Finally, scholars of fascism themselves bring to their studies different political and cultural attitudes, which often have a bearing on the importance they assign to one or another aspect of fascist ideology or practice. Secular liberals, for example, have stressed fascism's religious roots; Roman Catholic and Protestant scholars have emphasized its secular origins; social conservatives have pointed to its "socialist" and "populist" aspects; and social radicals have noted its defense of "capitalism" and "elitism."

Benito Mussolini

An unruly but intelligent youth, Benito Mussolini (b. July 29, 1883, Predappio, Italy–d. April 28, 1945, near Dongo) was the first child of the local blacksmith. In later years he expressed pride in his humble origins and often spoke of himself as a "man of the people." The Mussolini family was, in fact, less humble than he claimed—his father, a part-time socialist journalist as well as a blacksmith, was the son of a lieutenant in the National Guard, and his mother was a schoolteacher— but the Mussolinis were certainly poor.

He read widely and voraciously, if not deeply, plunging into the philosophers and theorists Immanuel Kant, Benedict de Spinoza, Peter Kropotkin, Friedrich Nietzsche, G.W.F. Hegel,
(continued on the next page)

Benito Mussolini. H. Roger-Viollet

Karl Kautsky, and Georges Sorel, picking out what appealed to him and discarding the rest, forming no coherent political philosophy of his own yet impressing his companions as a potential revolutionary of uncommon personality and striking presence. While earning a reputation as a political journalist and public speaker, he produced propaganda for a trade union, proposing a strike and advocating violence as a means of enforcing demands. Repeatedly, he called for a day of vengeance. More than once he was arrested and imprisoned. When he returned to Italy in 1904, even the Roman newspapers had started to mention his name.

Mussolini became an ardent socialist and served as editor of the party newspaper, *Avanti!* (1912–14). As its antimilitarist, antinationalist, and anti-imperialist editor, he thunderously opposed Italy's intervention in World War I. When he reversed his opposition to World War I, he was ousted by the party.

He founded the pro-war *Il Popolo d'Italia*, served with the Italian army (1915–17), then returned to his editorship. Advocating government by dictatorship, he formed a political group in 1919 that marked the beginning of fascism. A dynamic and captivating orator at rallies, he organized the March on Rome (1922) to prevent a socialist-led general strike. After the government fell, he was appointed prime minister, the youngest in Italian history. He obtained a law to establish the fascists as the majority party and became known as *Il Duce* ("The Leader"). He restored order to the country and introduced social reforms and public works improvements that won widespread popular support. His dreams of empire led to the invasion of Abyssinia (later Ethiopia) in 1935.

Supported in his fascist schemes by Adolf Hitler but wary of German power, Mussolini agreed to the Rome-Berlin Axis and declared war on the Allies in 1940. Italian military defeats in Greece and North Africa led to growing disillusionment with Mussolini. After the Allied invasion of Sicily (1943), the Fascist Grand Council dismissed him from office. He was arrested and imprisoned but rescued by German commandos, then became head of the Hitler-installed puppet government at Salò in northern Italy. As German defenses in Italy collapsed in 1945, Mussolini tried to escape to Austria but was captured and executed by Italian partisans.

For these and other reasons, there is no universally accepted definition of fascism. Nevertheless, it is possible to identify a number of general characteristics that fascist movements between 1922 and 1945 tended to have in common.

Opposition to Marxism

Fascists made no secret of their hatred of Marxists of all stripes, from totalitarian communists to democratic socialists. Fascists promised to deal more "firmly" with Marxists than had earlier, more democratic rightist parties. Mussolini first made his reputation as a fascist by unleashing armed squads of Blackshirts on striking workers and peasants in 1920–21. Many early Nazis had served in the Freikorps, the paramilitary groups formed by ex-soldiers to suppress leftist activism in Germany at the end of World War I. The Nazi SA (*Sturmabteilung* ["Assault Division"], or Brownshirts) clashed regularly with German leftists in the streets before 1933, and when Hitler came to power he sent hundreds of Marxists to concentration camps and intimidated "red" neighbourhoods with police raids and beatings.

For French fascists, Marxism was the main enemy. In 1925, Valois, leader of the Faisceau, declared that the guiding principle of his organization was "the elimination of socialism and everything resembling it." In 1926 Taittinger declared that the primary goal of his Patriotic Youth was to "defeat the progress of communism by any means necessary," adding that "We defend the hierarchy of classes....Everyone knows that there will always be different social levels, the strong and the weak, the rich and the poor, the governing and the governed." In 1936 French Popular Party leader Doriot announced that "Our politics are simple. We want a union of the French people against Marxism." Similarly, Colonel François de La Rocque, head of the Cross of Fire/French Social Party, warned that communism was "the danger par excellence" and that the machinations of Moscow were threatening France with "insurrection, subversion, catastrophe."

In 1919–20 the Heimwehr in Austria performed the same function that the Freikorps did in Germany, its volunteer militia units (*Heimatschutz*) doing battle with perceived foreign enemies and the Marxist foe within. Many of these units were organized by members of the landed gentry and the middle class to counter strikes by workers in the industrial districts of Linz and Steyer. In 1927 violent clashes between the Heimwehr and the Schutzbund, a socialist defense organization, resulted in many deaths and injuries among the leftists. In 1934 the Heimwehr joined Engelbert Dollfuss's Fatherland Front and was instrumental in pushing Dollfuss toward fascism.

Engelbert Dollfuss

Engelbert Dollfuss (b. Oct. 4, 1892, Texing, Austro-Hungarian Empire–d. July 25, 1934, Vienna, Austria) was an Austrian statesman and, from 1932 to 1934, chancellor of Austria, who destroyed the Austrian Republic and established an authoritarian regime based on conservative Roman Catholic and Italian Fascist principles.

After studying law and economics in Vienna and Berlin, Dollfuss became secretary to the Lower Austrian Peasant Federation and, in 1927, director of the Lower Austrian chamber of agriculture. He was a member of the conservative and clerically oriented Christian Social Party, the core of whose constituency came from Austria's conservative peasantry. Dollfuss rose rapidly in Austrian politics, serving as president of the federal railways in 1930 and as minister of agriculture from 1931. In May 1932 he became chancellor, heading a conservative coalition led by the Christian Social Party.

Faced with a severe economic crisis caused by the Great Depression, Dollfuss decided against joining Germany in a customs union, a course advocated by many Austrians. He was in part dissuaded by a League of Nations loan of $9,000,000

(continued on the next page)

and by the fear of Allied countermeasures. Severely criticized by Social Democrats, Pan-German nationalists, and Austrian Nazis, he countered by drifting toward an increasingly authoritarian regime. The Italian leader Benito Mussolini became his principal foreign ally. Italy guaranteed Austrian independence at Riccione (August 1933), but in return Austria had to abolish all political parties and reform its constitution on the Fascist model. Dollfuss's attacks on Parliament, begun in March 1933, culminated that September in the permanent abolition of the legislature and the formation of a corporate state based on his Vaterländische Front ("Fatherland Front"), with which he expected to replace Austria's political parties. In foreign affairs he steered a course that converted Austria virtually into an Italian satellite state. Hoping therewith to prevent Austria's incorporation into Nazi Germany, he fought his domestic political opponents along fascist-authoritarian lines.

In February 1934 paramilitary formations loyal to the chancellor crushed Austria's Social Democrats in bloody encounters. With a new constitution of May 1934, his regime became completely dictatorial. In June, however, Germany incited the Austrian Nazis to civil war. Dollfuss was assassinated by the Nazis in a raid on the chancellery.

Many Finnish fascists began their political careers after World War I as members of the anticommunist paramilitary group the White Guards. In Spain much of the Falange's early violence was directed against socialist students at the University of Madrid. Portuguese Blue Shirts, who called themselves "national syndicalists," regarded systematic violence against leftists to be "revolutionary." During the Spanish Civil War, Spanish, Portuguese, Italian, and German fascists joined forces to defeat the Popular Front, a coalition of liberals, socialists, communists, and anarchists who had been democratically elected in 1936.

In 1919 a number of fascist groups emerged in Japan to resist new demands for democracy and to counter the influence of the Russian Revolution of 1917. Although there were important differences between these groups, they all opposed "bolshevization," which some Japanese fascists associated with increasing agitation by tenant farmers and industrial workers. Fascists acted as strikebreakers; launched violent assaults on left-wing labour unions, peasant unions, and the socialist Levelling Society; and disrupted May Day celebrations. In 1938 Japanese fascists, having become powerful in the national government, supported the mass arrest of leaders of the General Council of Trade Unions (Nihon Rodo Kumiai So Hyogikai) and the Japan Proletarian Party (Dai Nippon Seisan-To) and of professors close to the Labour-Peasant Faction. Celebrations of May Day in Japan were prohibited in 1938, and in 1939 Japan withdrew from all international labour organizations.

Despite the fascists' violent opposition to Marxism, some observers have noted significant similarities between fascism and Soviet communism. Both were mass movements, both emerged in the years following World War I in circumstances of political turmoil and economic collapse, both sought to create totalitarian systems after they came to power (and often concealed their totalitarian ambitions beforehand), and both employed terror and violence without scruple when it was expedient to do so. Other scholars have cautioned against reading too much into these similarities, however, noting that fascist regimes (in particular Nazi Germany) used terror for different purposes and against different groups than did the Soviets and that fascists, unlike communists, generally supported capitalism and defended the interests of economic elites.

Fascist movements criticized parliamentary democracy for allowing the Marxist threat to exist in the first place.

According to Hitler, democracy undermined the natural selection of ruling elites and was "nothing other than the systematic cultivation of human failure." Joseph Goebbels, Hitler's minister of propaganda, maintained that the people never rule themselves and claimed that every history-making epoch had been created by aristocrats. Primo de Rivera wrote that "our Spain will not emerge from elections" but would be saved by poets with "weapons in their hands." In Japan the Tojo dictatorship dissolved all political parties, even right-wing groups, and reduced other political freedoms.

Before they came to power, Hitler and Mussolini, despite their dislike of democracy, were willing to engage in electoral politics and give the appearance of submitting to democratic procedures. When Hitler was appointed chancellor in 1933, he abandoned his military uniform for a civilian suit and bowed profusely to President Paul von Hindenburg in public ceremonies. In 1923 Mussolini proposed an electoral reform, known as the Acerbo Law, that gave two-thirds of the seats in Parliament to the party that received the largest number of votes. Although Mussolini insisted that he wanted to save Parliament rather than undermine it, the Acerbo Law enabled the fascists to take control of Parliament the following year and impose a dictatorship.

In France, La Rocque declared in 1933 that no election should take place without a preliminary "cleansing of [government] committees and the press," and he threatened to use his paramilitary squads to silence "agitators of disorder." In 1935 he called elections exercises in "collective decadence," and early in 1936 he told his followers that "even the idea of soliciting a vote nauseates me." A few months later, faced with the prospect that the Cross of Fire would be banned by the government as a paramilitary organization, he founded a new and ostensibly more democratic party, the French Social Party, which he publicly claimed was "firmly attached to republican liberties." He privately made it clear to his followers, however, that his conversion was more tactical than principled: "To scorn universal suffrage," he said, "does not withstand examination. Neither Mussolini nor Hitler...committed that mistake. Hitlerism, in particular, raised itself to total power through elections." With the collapse of the Third Republic in 1940 and the creation of the Vichy regime, La Rocque returned to condemning democracy as he had before 1936: "The world situation has put a halt to democracy," he wrote. "We have condemned the thing as well as the word." In 1941 La Rocque insisted that the French people obey Vichy's new leaders the way soldiers obeyed their officers.

Opposition to Political and Cultural Liberalism

Although circumstances sometimes made accommodation to political liberalism necessary, fascists condemned this doctrine for placing the rights of the individual above the needs of the *Volk*, encouraging "divisiveness" (i.e., political pluralism), tolerating "decadent" values, and limiting the power of the state. Fascists accused liberal "fellow travelers" of wittingly or unwittingly abetting communism. In 1935 the Cross of Fire berated "moderates"—i.e., democratic conservatives—for indirectly aiding the communists through their taste for "compromise and hesitation." La Rocque urged the French people to stand up against revolution and its "sordid ally" moderation, warning that, on the final day of reckoning, complicit moderates— "guardians unfaithful to their charge"—would be "at the head of the list of the guilty."

Fascist propagandists also attacked cultural liberalism, claiming that it encouraged moral relativism, godless materialism, and selfish individualism and thereby undermined traditional morality. Anti-Semitic fascists associated liberalism with Jews in particular—indeed, one precursor of Nazism, the political theorist Theodor Fritsch, claimed that to succumb to a liberal idea was to succumb to the Jew within oneself.

Totalitarian Ambitions

Although Hitler had not revealed the full extent of his totalitarian aims before he came to power, as Führer ("Leader") of the Third Reich, he attempted not only to control all political power but also to dominate many institutions and organizations that were previously independent of the state, such as courts, churches, universities, social clubs, veterans groups, sports associations, and youth groups. Even the German family came under assault, as members of the Hitler Youth were told that it was their patriotic duty to inform on anti-Nazi parents. In Italy, Mussolini adopted the title of *duce* ("leader"), and his regime created billboards displaying slogans such as "The Duce is always right" (*Il Duce ha sempre ragione*) and "Believe, obey, fight" (*Credere, obbedire, combattere*). It should be noted that, despite their considerable efforts in this direction, neither Hitler nor Mussolini succeeded in creating a completely totalitarian regime. Indeed, both regimes were riven by competing and heterogeneous power groups (which Hitler and Mussolini played off against each other), and the fascists in Italy were significantly limited by the wishes of traditional elites, including the Catholic Church.

Before fascists came to power, however, they often disavowed totalitarian aims. This was especially true in countries such as France, where conservatives were alarmed by reports of the repression of dissident conservatives in Fascist Italy and Nazi Germany. After Hitler's crackdown on Roman Catholic dissidents in Germany in 1934 and 1935, French fascists took pains to deny that they were totalitarians, lest they alienate potential Catholic supporters in France. Indeed, they attacked "statism" and advocated a more decentralized government that would favour local economic elites. However, La Rocque's claim in 1936 that he supported republican liberties did not prevent him in 1941 from demanding "unanimity" under French general and national hero Philippe Pétain and a purge of practitioners of Freemasonry from all government departments.

Conservative Economic Programs

There were a few, usually small, fascist movements whose social and economic goals were left or left-centrist. Hendrik de Man in Belgium and Marcel Déat in France, both former socialists, were among those who hoped eventually to achieve a fairer distribution of wealth by appealing to fascist nationalism and class conciliation. In Poland the Camp of National Radicalism (Oboz Narodowo-Raykalny) supported land reform and the nationalization of industry, and fascists in Libya and Syria advocated Arab socialism. In Japan, Kita Ikki, an early theorist of Japanese fascism, called for the nationalization of large industries, a limited degree of worker control, and a modern welfare program for the poor.

However, the economic programs of the great majority of fascist movements were extremely conservative, favouring the wealthy far more than the middle class and the working class. Their talk of national "socialism" was quite fraudulent in this respect. Although some workers were duped by it before the fascists came to power, most remained loyal to the traditional antifascist parties of the left. As historian John Weiss noted, "Property and income distribution and the traditional class structure remained roughly the same under fascist rule. What changes there were favored the old elites or certain segments of the party leadership." Historian Roger Eatwell concurred: "If a revolution is understood to mean a significant shift in class relations, including a redistribution of income and wealth, there was no Nazi revolution."

Mussolini, a leading member of the Italian Socialist Party (Partito Socialista Italiano) before World War I, became a fierce antisocialist after the war. After coming to power, he banned all Marxist organizations and replaced their trade unions with government-controlled corporatist unions. Until he instituted a war economy in the mid-1930s, Mussolini allowed industrialists to run their companies with a minimum of government interference. Despite his former anticapitalist rhetoric, he cut taxes on business, permitted cartel growth, decreed wage reduction, and rescinded the eight-hour-workday law. Between 1928 and 1932 real wages in Italy dropped by almost half. Mussolini admitted that the standard of living had fallen but stated that "fortunately the Italian people were not accustomed to eating much and therefore feel the privation less acutely than others."

Although Hitler claimed that the Nazi Party was more "socialist" than its conservative rivals, he opposed any Marxist-inspired nationalization of major industries. On May 2, 1933, he abolished all free trade unions in Germany, and his minister of labour, Robert Ley, later declared that it was necessary "to restore absolute leadership to the natural leader of the factory, that is, the employer." Nazi "anticapitalism," such as it was, was aimed primarily at Jewish capitalism; non-Jewish capitalists were allowed to keep their companies and their wealth, a distinction that was made in the Nazi Party's original program and never changed. Although Hitler reduced unemployment in Germany, most German workers were forced to toil for lower wages and longer hours and under worse conditions than had been the case during the Weimar Republic. His solution to the unemployment problem also depended on the recruitment of thousands of men into the military.

Corporatism

The fascist economic theory corporatism called for organizing each of the major sectors of industry, agriculture, the professions, and the arts into state- or management-controlled trade unions and employer associations, or "corporations," each of which would negotiate labour contracts and working conditions and represent the general interests of their professions in a larger assembly of corporations, or "corporatist parliament." Corporatist institutions would replace all independent organizations of workers and employers, and the corporatist parliament would replace, or at least exist alongside, traditional representative and legislative bodies. In theory, the corporatist model represented a "third way" between capitalism and communism, allowing for the harmonious cooperation of workers and employers for the good of the nation as a whole. In practice, fascist corporatism was used to destroy labour movements and suppress political dissent. In 1936, for example, the economic program of the French Social Party included shorter working hours and vacations with pay for "loyal" workers but not for "disloyal" ones, and benefits were to be assigned by employers, not the government. The Nazi "Strength Through Joy" program, which provided subsidies for vacations and other leisure activities for workers, operated on similar principles.

Extensive corporatist legislation was passed in Italy beginning in the late 1920s, creating several government-controlled unions and outlawing strikes. The Salazar regime in Portugal, using the Italian legislation as its model, outlawed the Trade Union Federation and all leftist unions, made corporatist unions compulsory for workers, and declared strikes illegal—all of which contributed to a decline in real wages. Croatian, Russian, Argentine, Brazilian, and Chilean fascism also proposed corporatist solutions to labour-management strife.

Alleged Equality of Social Status

In the political discourse of the fascist right, economic problems related to large disparities of wealth between rich and poor were treated as problems of social status and class prejudice. Rather than attacking upper-class wealth, fascists attacked upper-class snobbism. Rather than narrowing class differences, they taught that these differences were subjective and unimportant. National "socialism" was said to occur when a Hitler Youth from a rich family and a Hitler Youth from a poor family became comrades; no wealth had to be shared. This conception of socialism was in part an outgrowth of the Nazis' attempt to transfer military values to civilian life: In war it did not matter if the soldier next to you came from a poor or a wealthy background as long as he fought loyally for the combat unit.

Imperialism

Many fascist movements had imperialistic aims. Hitler hoped that his *Drang nach Osten* ("drive toward the east"), by conquering Eastern Europe and Russia, would not only prove the racial superiority of Aryans over Slavs but also provide enough plunder and *Lebensraum* ("living space") to overcome continuing economic difficulties at home. Mussolini's imperial ambitions were directed at North Africa, and his armies invaded Ethiopia in 1935. Polish fascists advocated retaking all the lands that had ever been ruled by Polish kings, including East Prussia. Finnish fascists wanted to create a "Greater Finland" at the expense of Russia, and Croatian fascists advocated a "Greater Croatia" at the expense of Serbia. Japanese fascists preached military conquest on behalf of their plan for a "Greater East Asia Co-Prosperity Sphere." French fascists were strong defenders of the French empire in Indochina and North Africa, and during the interwar period they attracted considerable support among the ruling European minority (*colons*) in Algeria. Portuguese fascists waged colonial wars in Guinea, Angola, and Mozambique. Syrian, Iraqi, and Egyptian fascist movements also supported territorial expansionism. However, there were some "peace fascisms" that were not imperialistic, such as the Integralist Action movement in Brazil.

Military Values

Fascists favoured military values such as courage, unquestioning obedience to authority, discipline, and physical strength. They also adapted the outward trappings of military organizations, such as paramilitary uniforms and Roman salutes. Hitler imagined a God who presided over military conflicts and ensured the survival of the fittest. Mussolini was famous for slogans such as "A minute on the battlefield is worth a lifetime of peace," "Better to live an hour like a lion than a hundred years like a sheep," and "Nothing has ever been won in history without bloodshed." Similarly, a pamphlet published by the Japanese War Ministry in 1934 declared: "War is the father of creation and the mother of culture." The songs of Spanish Falangists extolled the nobility of death in war. Like many fascists, the French writer Pierre Drieu La Rochelle, author of the fascist novel *Gilles*, prided himself on his "tough-minded" realism, which accepted killing as a principle of nature. La Rocque's organization, originally a war veterans' movement, prided itself on the martial "spirit of the Cross of Fire," and its spokesmen made nefarious comparisons between "virile" combat soldiers and "decadent" civilian politicians.

Volksgemeinschaft

Hitler envisioned the ideal German society as a *Volksgemeinschaft*, a racially unified and hierarchically organized body in which the interests of individuals would be strictly subordinate to those of the nation, or Volk. Like a military battalion, the people's community would be permanently prepared for war and would accept the discipline that this required. The Italian, French, and Spanish versions of this doctrine, known as "integral nationalism," were similarly illiberal, though not racist. The Japanese version, known as the "family-system principle," maintained that the nation is like a family: it is strong only when the people obey their leaders in the same way children obey their parents.

Mass Mobilization

Fascists characteristically attempted to win popular support and consolidate their power by mobilizing the population in mass meetings, parades, and other gatherings. Exploiting principles borrowed from modern American advertising, which stressed the importance of appealing to the audience's emotions rather than to its reason, fascists used such gatherings to create patriotic fervour and to encourage fanatic enthusiasm for the fascist cause. The Nazi rallies at Nürnberg, for example, were organized with theatrical precision and featured large banners, paramilitary uniforms, martial music, torchlight parades, bonfires, and forests of fascist salutes accompanied by prompted shouts of "Sieg Heil!" Hitler believed it best to hold such gatherings at night, when audiences would be more susceptible to irrational appeals than in the daytime. Fascists also sought to regiment the population, especially young people, by infiltrating local social networks—tavern groups and veteran, sports, church, student, and other organizations—and providing soup kitchens, vacation outings, and nationalistic ceremonies for townspeople. In France, La Rocque's French Social Party dispensed meals to the unemployed and offered workers access to swimming

Nazi storm troopers displaying large banners while marching through Nürnberg, Germany, where many such rallies took place at various times between 1923 and 1938 in an effort to promote popular support for the Nazi cause. © AP Images

pools, social clubs, and vacation grounds in order to entice them into the movement.

Mussolini's regime in Italy and Salazar's government in Portugal also held government-organized mass rallies. After 1936 Japanese fascists paid less attention to mass mobilization than to working directly with the nation's elites. The dictatorship that followed was based on a coalition of military leaders, industrialists, state bureaucrats, and conservative party politicians.

The Leadership Principle

Fascists defended the *Führerprinzip* ("leadership principle"), the belief that the party and the state should have a single leader with absolute power. Hitler was the Führer and Mussolini the Duce, both words for the "leader" who gave the orders that everyone else had to obey. The authority of the leader was often enhanced by his personal charisma.

The leadership principle was also conceived to apply at lower levels of the political and social hierarchy. Fascist organizations sometimes exhibited the so-called "corporal syndrome," in which persons willingly submit to the authority of those above them in exchange for the gratification they derive from dominating those below. Japanese fascists believed that owners of stores and workshops should exercise "paternal" authority over their assistants, clerks, workers, servants, and tenants. Subordinates were not permitted to organize themselves into unions, and the small bosses assumed the leadership of town and village councils. As historian Masao Maruyama notes, this mind-set affected the way many Japanese shop masters viewed their nation's foreign policy in the 1930s: "The resistance of the East Asian peoples to Japanese imperialism aroused the same psychological reactions among them as the resistance of their subordinates in the shops, workplaces, and other groups under

Führer

Führer (also spelled Fuehrer, German *Führer* ["Leader"]) refers to the title used by Adolf Hitler to define his role of absolute authority in Germany's Third Reich (1933–45). As early as July 1921 he had declared the *Führerprinzip* ("leader principle") to be the law of the Nazi Party; and in *Mein Kampf* (1925–27) he asserted that such a dictatorship would be extended to the coming Third Reich.

A personality cult was built around the Führer. Hitler's portraits and photographs were displayed everywhere in Germany. "Heil Hitler!" ("Hail Hitler!") became legally obligatory as a common greeting, as did the Hitler salute of the right arm fully thrust forward with the palm facing downward.

Organizationally, the Führer stood at the apex of a hierarchy. Directly below him were several *Reichsleiter* ("Reich leaders") with various portfolios, such as finance, propaganda, foreign policy, and law, as well as *Reichsführer* Heinrich Himmler, head of the unified police system. Also directly responsible to (and selected by) the Führer were many territorial leaders (43 in greater Germany) known as *Gauleiter* ("district leaders").

their control. Thus they became the most ardent supporters of the China Incident [the Mukden Incident (1931), in which Japanese troops seized the Manchurian city of Mukden] and the Pacific War."

The "New Man"

Fascists aimed to transform the ordinary man into the "new man," a "virile" being who would put decadent bourgeoisie, cerebral Marxists, and "feminine" liberals to shame. The new man would be physically strong and morally "hard," admiring what was forceful and vigorous and despising everything "weak" and "soft." As Hitler described him, the new man was "slim and slender, quick like a greyhound, tough like leather, and hard like Krupp steel." The new man was a man of the past as well as the future. Italian fascists held up the soldiers of ancient Rome as models, and Bertrand de Jouvenel praised the "brutal barons" of the Middle Ages and the original conquerors of Europe, the Franks. "Fascist man," he wrote, was "a throwback to the warrior and property holder of yesteryear, to the type of man who was the head of a family and a clan: When this type of man ceases to win esteem and disappears, then the process of decadence begins."

Drieu La Rochelle believed Hitlerian man to be superior to Democratic man, Marxist man, and Liberal man. "The Hitlerian," he wrote, "is a type who rejects culture, who stands firm in the middle of sexual and alcoholic depravity and who dreams of bringing to the world a physical discipline with radical effects." The new man was also a Darwinian "realist" who was contemptuous of "delicate" souls who refused to employ harsh military or political measures when they were required.

During World War II, in a speech to an SS unit that had executed many Jews, SS chief Heinrich Himmler reminded his "new men" that they needed to be emotionally as well as physically hard: "Most of you know what it means when 100 corpses are piled up, when 500 or 1,000 are piled there. To have gone through this and—with exceptions due to weakness—to have remained decent, that is what has made us hard. I have to expect of you superhuman acts of inhumanity....We have no right to be weak....[Our men] must never be soft. They must grit their teeth and do their duty."

Glorification of Youth

Fascists praised the young for their physical strength and honoured them for their idealism and spirit of self-sacrifice—

qualities, they said, that were often lacking in their elders. Fascists often presented their cause in generational terms. As the young Goebbels declared, "The old ones don't even want to understand that we young people even exist. They defend their power to the last. But one day they will be defeated after all. Youth finally must be victorious." De Jouvenel described fascism as a "revolution of the body" that reflected youth's hunger for discipline, effort, combat, and courage. The young, who loved "strong and slender bodies, vigorous and sure movements, [and] short sentences," consequently detested middle-aged, pot-bellied liberals and café verbosity.

Adolf Hitler meeting with members of the Hitler Youth, an organization dedicated to training male youth in principles of the Nazi Party. Heinrich Hoffmann/Time & Life Pictures/Getty Images

Partly because they made concerted appeals to young people, fascist parties tended to have younger members than most other rightist parties. The leadership of the Nazi Party, for example, was relatively young, and junior officers in the German army often went over to fascism sooner than senior officers. Corneliu Codreanu, leader of the Iron Guard in Romania, was only 31 when he founded the movement in 1930, and his major lieutenants were in their 20s. Similarly, José Antonio Primo de Rivera was only 30 when he founded the Falange in Spain, and in 1936, 60 to 70 percent of his followers were under 21.

Education as Character Building

Fascist educators emphasized character building over intellectual growth, devalued the transmission of information, inculcated blind obedience to authority, and discouraged critical and independent thinking that challenged fascist ideology. According to Nazi writer Herman Klaus, the teacher "is not just an instructor and transmitter of knowledge.... He is a soldier, serving on the cultural and political front of National Socialism. For intellectuals belong to the people or they are nothing." The ultimate aim of Nazi education was not to make students think more richly but to make them war more vigorously. As the Nazi minister of culture in Prussia wrote, "The National Socialist revolution has replaced the image of the cultivated personality with the reality of the true German man. It has substituted for the humanistic conception of culture a system of education which develops out of the fellowship of actual battle." Teachers who did not practice these principles or who appeared skeptical of Nazi "idealism" were subject to dismissal, often as a result of reports by student informers.

Decadence and Spirituality

Some of the ugliest aspects of fascism—intolerance, repression, and violence—were fueled by what fascists saw as a morally justified struggle against "decadence." For fascists, decadence meant a number of things: materialism, self-indulgence, hedonism, cowardice, and physical and moral softness. It was also associated with rationalism, skepticism, atheism, humanitarianism, and political, economic, and gender democracy, as well as rule by the Darwinian unfit, by the weak and the "female." For anti-Semitic fascists, Jews were the most decadent of all.

The opposite of decadence was "spirituality," which transcended materialism and generated self-discipline and virility. The spiritual attitude involved a certain emotional asceticism that enabled one to avoid feelings of pity for one's victims. It also involved Darwinian notions of survival of the fittest, a belief in the right of natural elites to upward social and political mobility, and accommodation with members of the upper classes. It prized hierarchy, respect for superiors, and military obedience. It was forceful toward the weak, and it was "male." The spiritual attitude was also hateful. In 1934 Ernst Röhm, leader of the SA, worried that Germans had "forgotten how to hate." "Virile hate," he wrote, "has been replaced by feminine lamentation. But he who is unable to hate cannot love either. Fanatical love and hate—their fires kindle flames of freedom." De Jouvenel agreed: "Any sentiment less vigorous than hatred indicates a lack of virility."

Violence

Fascists reacted to their opponents with physical force. Primo de Rivera maintained that "no other argument is admissible than that of fists and pistols when justice or the Fatherland is

Blackshirt

A Blackshirt (Italian: *Camicia Nera*, plural: *Camicie Nere*) was a member of any of the armed squads of Italian Fascists under Benito Mussolini, who wore black shirts as part of their uniform.

The first squads—each of which was called *Squadre d'Azione* ("Action Squad")—were organized in March 1919 to destroy the political and economic organizations of socialists. By the end of 1920 the Blackshirts were attacking and destroying the organizations not only of socialists but also of communists, republicans, Catholics, trade unionists, and those in cooperatives, and hundreds of people were killed as the fascist squads expanded in number. A fascist convention in Naples on Oct. 24, 1922, provided the pretext for the concentration of armed Blackshirts from all over the country for the famous March on Rome that put Mussolini into power.

A squad of Italian Blackshirts wearing their trademark uniforms standing in formation. FPG/Archive Photos/Getty Images

Early the next year, on Feb. 1, 1923, the private Blackshirts were officially transformed into a national militia, the Voluntary Fascist Militia for National Security. The black shirt was worn not only by these military fascists but also by other fascists and their sympathizers, especially on patriotic occasions. With the fall of Mussolini in 1943, however, the black shirt and the Blackshirts fell into disgrace.

attacked." Before he came to power, Mussolini sent his Blackshirts to assault socialist organizers throughout Italy, and later he sent many leftists to prison. Hitler's storm troopers served a similar function, and Nazi concentration camps at first interned more Marxists than Jews. Nor were dissident conservatives spared Nazi violence. Hitler's infamous "Blood Purge" of June 1934, in which Röhm and other SA leaders were summarily executed, also claimed the lives of Kurt von Schleicher, the last chancellor of the Weimar Republic, and his wife, who were murdered in their home. To his critics Hitler replied, "People accuse us of being barbarians; we are barbarians, and we are proud of it!" In Romania, Codreanu's "death teams" engaged in brutal strikebreaking, and, in France, Drieu La Rochelle glorified military and political violence as healthy antidotes to decadence. Beginning in 1931 Japanese fascists assassinated a number of important political figures, but in 1936, after a government crackdown, they renounced such tactics. In the United States in the 1920s and '30s, the Ku Klux Klan and other groups sought to intimidate African Americans with cross burnings, beatings, and lynchings.

Extreme Nationalism

Whereas cosmopolitan conservatives often supported international cooperation and admired elite culture in other countries, fascists espoused extreme nationalism and cultural parochialism. Fascist ideologues taught that national identity was the foundation of individual identity and should not be corrupted by foreign influences, especially if they were left-wing. Nazism condemned Marxist and liberal internationalisms as threats to German national unity. Fascists in general wanted to replace internationalist class solidarity with nationalist class collaboration. The Italian, French, and Spanish notion of integral nationalism was hostile to individualism and political pluralism. Unlike democratic conservatives, fascists accused their political opponents of being less "patriotic" than they, sometimes even labeling them "traitors." Portuguese fascists spoke of "internal foreigners" who were "antination." In the 1930s some French fascist organizations even rejected the label "fascist," lest they be perceived as beholden to Germany.

In France, immigrants—particularly left-wing immigrants—were special targets of fascist nationalism. Jean Renaud of French Solidarity demanded that all foreigners seeking residence in France be rigorously screened and that the unfit be denied entry "without pity"—especially social revolutionaries, who made France "not a refuge for the oppressed but a depository for trash." In 1935 La Rocque blamed Hitler for driving German refugees into France and condemned the "foolish sentimentality" that prompted the government to accept them. He also criticized France's naturalization policies for allowing cities like Marseille and Paris to be inundated by a rising tide of "undesirables." France, he declared, had become the shepherd of "a swarming, virulent mob of *outlaws*," some of whom, under the pretext of fleeing Nazi persecution, were really infiltrating France as spies.

Scapegoating

Fascists often blamed their countries' problems on scapegoats. Jews, Freemasons, Marxists, and immigrants were

Nationalism

Nationalism is an ideology based on the premise that the individual's loyalty and devotion to the nation-state surpass other individual or group interests.

Nationalism is a modern movement. Throughout history people have been attached to their native soil, to the traditions of their parents, and to established territorial authorities; but it was not until the end of the 18th century that nationalism began to be a generally recognized sentiment molding public and private life and one of the great, if not the greatest, single determining factors of modern history. Because of its dynamic vitality and its all-pervading character, nationalism is often thought to be very old; sometimes it is mistakenly regarded as a permanent factor in political behaviour. Actually, the American and French revolutions may be regarded as its first powerful manifestations. After penetrating the new countries of Latin America it spread in the early 19th century to central Europe and from there, toward the middle of the century, to Eastern and Southeastern Europe. At the beginning of the 20th century nationalism flowered in the ancient lands of Asia and Africa. Thus the 19th century has been called the age of nationalism in Europe, while the 20th century has witnessed the rise and struggle of powerful national movements throughout Asia and Africa.

Nationalism, translated into world politics, implies the identification of the state or nation with the people—or at least the desirability of determining the extent of the state according to ethnographic principles. In the age of nationalism, but only in the age of nationalism, the principle was generally recognized that each nationality should form a state—its state—and that the state should include all members of that nationality. Formerly states, or territories under one administration, were not delineated by nationality. Men did not give their loyalty to the nation-state but to other, different forms of political organization: the city-state,

(continued on the next page)

the feudal fief and its lord, the dynastic state, the religious group, or the sect. The nation-state was nonexistent during the greater part of history, and for a very long time it was not even regarded as an ideal.

Before the 18th century there had been evidences of national feeling among certain groups at certain periods, especially in times of stress and conflict. The rise of national feeling to major political importance was encouraged by a number of complex developments: the creation of large, centralized states ruled by absolute monarchs who destroyed the old feudal allegiances; the secularization of life and of education, which fostered the vernacular languages and weakened the ties of church and sect; and the growth of commerce, which demanded larger territorial units to allow scope for the dynamic spirit of the rising middle classes and their capitalistic enterprise. This large, unified territorial state, with its political and economic centralization, became imbued in the 18th century with a new spirit—an emotional fervour similar to that of religious movements in earlier periods. Under the influence of the new theories of the sovereignty of the people and the rights of man, the people replaced the king as the centre of the nation. No longer was the king the nation or the state; the state had become the people's state, a national state, a fatherland. State became identified with nation, as civilization became identified with national civilization.

German nationalism began to stress instinct against reason; the power of historical tradition against rational attempts at progress and a more just order; the historical differences between nations rather than their common aspirations. The French Revolution, liberalism, and equality were regarded as a brief aberration, against which the eternal foundations of societal order would prevail. That German interpretation was shown to be false by the developments of the 19th century. Liberal nationalism reasserted itself and affected more and more people: the rising middle class and the new proletariat. The revolutionary wave of 1848, the year of "the spring of the peoples," seemed to realize the hopes of nationalists such as Giuseppe Mazzini, who had devoted his life to the unification of the Italian nation by democratic means and to the brotherhood of all free nations. Though his immediate hopes were disappointed, the 12 years from 1859 to 1871 brought the unification of Italy and Romania, both with the help of Napoleon III, and of Germany; at the same time the 1860s saw great progress in liberalism, even in Russia and Spain. The victorious trend of liberal nationalism, however, was reversed in Germany by Bismarck. He unified Germany on a conservative and authoritarian basis and defeated German liberalism. The German annexation of Alsace-Lorraine against the will of the inhabitants was contrary to the idea of nationalism as based upon the free will of man. The people of Alsace-Lorraine were held to be German by objective factors, by race, independent of their will or of their allegiance to any nationality of their choice.

In the second half of the 19th century, nationalism disintegrated the supranational states of the Habsburgs and the Ottoman sultans, both of which were based upon prenational loyalties. In Russia, the penetration of nationalism produced two opposing schools of thought. Some nationalists proposed a westernized Russia, associated with the progressive, liberal forces of the rest of Europe. Others stressed the distinctive character of Russia and Russianism, its independent and different destiny based upon its autocratic and orthodox past. These Slavophiles, similar to and influenced by German romantic thinkers, saw Russia as a future saviour of a West undermined by liberalism and the heritage of the American and French revolutions.

One of the consequences of World War I was the triumph of nationalism in Central and Eastern Europe. From the ruins of the Habsburg and Romanov empires emerged the new nation-states of Austria, Hungary, Czechoslovakia, Poland, Yugoslavia, and Romania. Those states in turn, however, were

(continued on the next page)

to be strained and ravaged by their own internal nationality conflicts and by nationalistic disputes over territory with their neighbours.

Russian nationalism was in part suppressed after Lenin's victory in 1917, when the Bolsheviks took over the old empire of the tsars. But the Bolsheviks also claimed the leadership of the world Communist movement, which was to become an instrument of the national policies of the Russians. During World War II Stalin appealed to nationalism and patriotism in rallying the Russians against foreign invaders. After the war he found nationalism one of the strongest obstacles to the expansion of Soviet power in Eastern Europe. National communism, as it was called, became a divisive force in the Soviet bloc. In 1948 Tito, the Communist leader of Yugoslavia, was denounced by Moscow as a nationalist and a renegade; nationalism was a strong factor in the rebellious movements in Poland and Hungary in the fall of 1956; and subsequently its influence was also felt in Romania and Czechoslovakia and again in Poland in 1980.

prominent among the groups that were demonized. According to fascist propaganda, the long depression of the 1930s resulted less from insufficient government regulation of the economy or inadequate lower-class purchasing power than from "Judeo-Masonic-bolshevik" conspiracies, left-wing agitation, and the presence of immigrants. The implication was that depriving these demons of their power and influence would cause the nation's major problems to go away.

Populism

Fascists praised the *Volk* and pandered to populist anti-intellectualism. Nazi art criticism, for example, upheld the populist view that the common man was the best judge of art and that art that did not appeal to popular taste was decadent. Also populist was the Nazi propaganda theme that Hitler was a "new man" who had "emerged from the depth of the people." Unlike left-wing populism, fascist populism did not attribute workers' hardships to big business and big landowners and did not advocate measures such as progressive taxation, higher pay for industrial and farm workers, protection of unions, and the right to strike.

A Nazi propaganda poster promoting the idea of a "new Germany." Universal Images Group/Getty Images

In general it spared the wealth of the upper classes—except that belonging to Jews.

Revolutionary Image

Fascists sometimes portrayed their movements as "new" and "revolutionary," an image that appealed not just to the young but to older literary modernists such as Filippo Marinetti, T.S. Eliot, Ezra Pound, Wyndham Lewis, William Butler

Yeats, D.H. Lawrence, and Paul de Man. However, dozens of fascist writers also praised cultural traditionalism, or "rootedness." Under the Third Reich, Goebbels subsidized an exhibition of modern art not to celebrate its glory but to expose its decadence; he called it simply the "Exhibition of Degenerate Art." Fascism's claims to newness did not prevent its propagandists from pandering to fearful traditionalists who associated cultural modernism with secular humanism, feminism, sexual license, and the destruction of the Christian family.

Antiurbanism

Fascists also pandered to antiurban feelings. The Nazis won most of their electoral support from rural areas and small towns. In Nazi propaganda the ideal German was not an urban intellectual but a simple peasant, and uprooted intellectualism was considered a threat to the deep, irrational sources of the *Volk* soul. Jews were often portrayed—and therefore condemned—as quintessential city dwellers. In 1941 La Rocque commented: "The theory of 'families of good stock who have their roots in the earth' leads us to conclusions not far from [those of] Walter Darre, Minister of Agriculture for the Reich." Romanian fascism relied heavily on the support of landed peasants who distrusted the "wicked" city. The agrarian wing of Japanese fascism praised the peasant soldier and denigrated the industrial worker.

Sexism and Misogyny

Under fascist regimes women were urged to perform their traditional gender role as wives and mothers and to bear many children for the nation. Mussolini instituted policies severely restricting women's access to jobs outside the home (policies that later had to be revised to meet wartime exigencies), and he distributed gold medals to mothers who produced the most children. In Germany the Nazis forbade female party members from giving orders to male members. In a speech in 1937, Charles Vallin, vice president of the French Social Party, equated feminists with insubordinate proletarians: "It is not with class struggle that the social question will be resolved. Yet, it is toward a sort of class struggle, opposing the feminine 'proletariat' to the masculine 'capitalist,' that feminism is leading us."

De Jouvenel equated women with hedonism and hedonism with decadence. Europe, he wrote in 1938, had grown soft and feminine from pleasure seeking, becoming "like a woman who had just escaped a frightening accident. [She] needed light, warmth, music." According to de Jouvenel, an atmosphere of "facility" corrupted everything, and people had become increasingly unwilling to take on painful tasks. In short, he believed the feminization of Europe had been its downfall. In a similar vein, Drieu La Rochelle claimed that educated women undermined his manhood. He characterized political movements he disliked as feminine and those he admired as masculine—fascism, for him, being the most masculine of all.

CHAPTER 3

ORIGINS OF FASCISM

Fascist parties and movements came to power in several countries between 1922 and 1945: the National Fascist Party (Partito Nazionale Fascista) in Italy, led by Mussolini; the National Socialist German Workers' Party (Nationalsozialistische Deutsche Arbeiterpartei), or Nazi Party, led by Adolf Hitler and representing his National Socialism movement; the Fatherland Front (Vaterländische Front) in Austria, led by Engelbert Dollfuss and supported by the Heimwehr (Home Defense Force), a major right-wing paramilitary organization; the National Union (União Nacional) in Portugal, led by António de Oliveira Salazar (which became fascist after 1936); the Party of Free Believers (Elefterofronoi) in Greece, led by Ioannis Metaxas; the Ustaša ("Insurgence") in Croatia, led by Ante Pavelic; the National Union (Nasjonal Samling) in Norway, which was in power for only a week—though its leader, Vidkun Quisling, was later made minister president under the German occupation; and the military dictatorship of Admiral Tojo Hideki in Japan.

Spain's fascist movement, the Falange ("Phalanx"), founded in 1933 by José Antonio Primo de Rivera, never came to power, but many of its members were absorbed into the military dictatorship of Francisco Franco, which itself displayed many fascist characteristics. In Poland the anti-Semitic Falanga, led by Boleslaw Piasecki, was influential but was unable to overthrow

Francisco Franco. Universal Images Group/Getty Images

the conservative regime of Józef Piłsudski. Vihtori Kosola's Lapua Movement in Finland nearly staged a coup in 1932 but was checked by conservatives backed by the army. The Arrow Cross Party (Nyilaskeresztes Párt) in Hungary, led by Ferenc Szálasi, was suppressed by the conservative regime of Miklós Horthy until 1944, when Szálasi was made a puppet ruler under the German occupation. In Romania the Iron Guard (Garda de Fier)—also called the League of Christian Defense, the Legion of the Archangel Michael, and All for the Fatherland— led by Corneliu Codreanu, was dissolved by the dictatorial regime of King Carol II in 1938. In 1939 Codreanu and several of his legionaries were arrested and "shot while trying to escape." In 1940 remnants of the Iron Guard reemerged to share power but were finally crushed by Romanian conservatives in February 1941.

Falange

The Falange (in full, *Falange Española* ["Spanish Phalanx"] or [1937–77] *Falange Española Tradicionalista y de las Juntas de Ofensiva Nacional-Sindicalista* ["Traditionalist Spanish Phalanx of the Juntas of the National Syndicalist Offensive"]) was an extreme nationalist political group founded in Spain in 1933 by José Antonio Primo de Rivera, son of the former dictator Miguel Primo de Rivera. Influenced by Italian fascism, the Falange joined forces (February 1934) with a like-minded group, Juntas de Ofensiva Nacional Sindicalista, and issued a manifesto of 27 points repudiating the republican constitution, party politics, capitalism, Marxism, and clericalism, and proclaiming the necessity of a national-syndicalist state, a strong government and military, and Spanish imperialist expansion.

Despite parades and strident proclamations, the Falange made little headway in its first three years. In the election of February 1936, which brought the Popular Front to power, the

Falange polled in Madrid only 5,000 votes out of a total right-wing vote of 180,000, and its only representative in the Cortes, Primo de Rivera himself, was defeated. With the coming to power of the Popular Front and the ensuing rapid polarization of Spanish politics, the Falangists gained increasing popularity at the expense of the conservatives and Roman Catholics of the right. Upon the military uprising against the Spanish Republic in July 1936, several of the Falange's principal leaders, including Primo de Rivera, were arrested and shot by Republican firing squads.

General Francisco Franco found in the Falange a potential political party and an explicit ideology at hand for his use. True, it had to be reconciled with traditionalist, clericalist, and monarchist elements within the Nationalist movement, but this was effected by the decree of April 19, 1937, whereby the Falange, the Carlists, and other right-wing factions were forcibly merged into one body with the cumbrous title of Falange Española Tradicionalista y de las Juntas de Ofensiva Nacional-Sindicalista. General Franco became the Falange's absolute chief and his brother-in-law Ramón Serrano Suñer its chief spokesman. The Falange's membership was over 250,000 when Franco seized control of it in 1937, and more than 150,000 Falangists served in Franco's armed forces during the Civil War.

After the victory of the Nationalists in 1939 and the end of the war, the Falange's radical fascist ideas were subordinated to the conservative and traditionalist values of Franco's regime. Membership in the Falange became indispensable to political advancement, but it gradually ceased to be identified with the original Falangist ideology as Franco's regime evolved during the late 1940s and '50s.

On Jan. 12, 1975, prior to Franco's death, a law was passed permitting the establishment of other "political associations"; thereafter and especially after Franco's death in November, other political parties began to proliferate. The Falange itself had become utterly moribund by this time and was formally abolished on April 1, 1977.

In France the Cross of Fire (Croix de Feu), later renamed the French Social Party (Parti Social Français), led by Colonel François de La Rocque, was the largest and fastest-growing party on the French right between 1936 and 1938. In 1937 it was larger than the French communist and socialist parties combined (one scholar estimated its membership between 700,000 and 1.2 million), and by 1939 it included some 3,000 mayors, about 1,000 municipal councilmen, and 12 parliamentary deputies. Other fascist movements in France included the short-lived Faisceau (1925–28), led by Georges Valois; the Young Patriots (Jeunesses Patriotes), led by Pierre Taittinger; French Solidarity (Solidarité Française), founded and financed by François Coty and led by Jean Renaud; the Franks (Francistes), led by Marcel Bucard; the French Popular Party (Parti Populaire Français), led by Jacques Doriot; and French Action (Action Française), led by Charles Maurras. After the German invasion in 1940, a number of French fascists served in the Vichy regime of Marshal Philippe Pétain.

The British Union of Fascists, led by Oswald Mosley, had some 50,000 members. In Belgium the Rexist Party, led by Léon Degrelle, won about 10 percent of the seats in the parliament in 1936. Russian fascist organizations were founded by exiles in Manchuria, the United States, and elsewhere; the largest of these groups were the Russian Fascist Party (VFP), led by Konstantin Rodzaevsky, and the All Russian Fascist Organization (VFO), led by Anastasy Vonsiatsky.

Outside Europe, popular support for fascism was greatest in South Africa and the Middle East. Several fascist groups were founded in South Africa after 1932, including the Gentile National Socialist Movement and its splinter group, the South African Fascists; the South African National Democratic Party, known as the Blackshirts; and the pro-German Ox-Wagon Sentinel (Ossewabrandwag). By 1939 there were at least seven Arab "shirt" movements, including the Syrian

People's Party, also called the Syrian National Socialist Party; the Iraqi Futuwa movement; and the Young Egypt movement, also called the Green Shirts.

Several rival protofascist and fascist movements operated in Japan after 1918, and their activities helped to increase the influence of the military on the Japanese government. Among the most important of these groups were the Taisho Sincerity League (Taisho Nesshin'kai), the Imperial Way Faction (Kodo-ha), the Greater Japan National Essence Association (Dai Nippon Kokusui-kai), the Anti-Red Corps (Bokyo Gokoku-Dan), the Great Japan Political Justice Corps (Dai Nippon Seigi-Dan), the Blood Brotherhood League (Ketsumei-Dan), the Jimmu Association (Jimmu-Kai), the New Japan League (Shin-Nihon Domei), the Eastern Way Society (Towo Seishin-Kai), and the Great Japan Youth Party (Da-nihon Seinen-dan).

Following the Mukden Incident, in which Japanese troops seized the Manchurian city of Mukden, and the wider invasion of Manchuria by Japanese troops in 1931, several fascist-oriented patriotic societies were formed in China; the largest of these groups, the Blue Shirts, formed an alliance with the Kuomintang (National People's Party) under Chiang Kai-shek. At Chiang's order in 1934, the Blue Shirts were temporarily put in charge of political indoctrination in the army and given limited control of its educational system.

European fascism had a number of imitators in Latin America, including the Nacis, founded in Chile by Jorge González von Mareés; the Gold Shirts, founded in Mexico by Nicolás Rodríguez; and the Revolutionary Union (Unión Revolucionaria) of Peruvian dictator Luis Sánchez Cerro. The Brazilian Integralist Action party (Ação Integralista Brasileira), which had some 200,000 members in the mid-1930s, was suppressed by the Brazilian government in 1938 after a failed coup attempt.

In the United States the Ku Klux Klan, a white supremacist organization founded at the end of the Civil War and revived in 1915, displayed some fascist characteristics. One of its offshoots, the Black Legion, had some 60,000 members in the early 1930s and committed numerous acts of arson and bombing. In 1930 Catholic priest Charles E. Coughlin began national radio broadcasts of sermons on political and economic subjects; his talks became increasingly antidemocratic and anti-Semitic, as did the journal he founded, *Social Justice*. After running unsuccessfully for the U.S. presidency in 1936, Coughlin became an apologist for Hitler, Mussolini, and Franco. In 1942 *Social Justice* was banned from the U.S. mail for violating the Espionage Act, and in the same year the American Catholic Church ordered Coughlin to stop his broadcasts. The pro-Nazi German-American Bund, founded in 1933, staged military drills and mass rallies until it disintegrated with the U.S. entry into the war in 1941.

Varieties of Fascism

Just as Marxists, liberals, and conservatives differed within and between various countries, so, too, did fascists. In some countries there were rivalries between native fascist movements over personal, tactical, and other differences. Fascist movements also displayed significant differences with respect to their acceptance of racism and particularly anti-Semitism, their identification with Christianity, and their support for Nazi Germany.

Acceptance of Racism

Although not all fascists believed in biological racism, it played a central role in the actions of those who did. Nazism was viciously racist, especially in its attitude toward Jews. The

Nazis blamed the Jews for almost everything wrong with Germany, from the Great Depression and the rise of Marxism to the evils of international capitalism and decadence in art. The Holocaust, culminating in the "final solution to the Jewish question," was the immensely cruel outcome of this hatred. From 1933 to 1945 some six million Jewish men, women, and children were exterminated by gassings, shootings, hangings, and clubbings, and about three million Slavs (whom the Nazis regarded as only slightly less racially inferior than Jews), as well as approximately 400,000 Gypsies (Roma), were murdered as well.

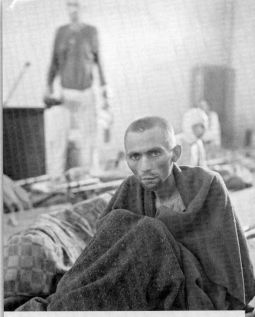

An inmate of a concentration camp at Gusen, Austria, suffering from starvation, May 12, 1945. T4c Sam Gilbert—Records of the Office of the Chief Signal Officer/ U.S. National Archives and Records Administration (111-SC- 264918)

Croatian fascists preached the racial inferiority of Serbs, and in the late 1930s they became increasingly anti-Semitic. When Germany invaded Yugoslavia in 1941, Ante Pavelic, the Ustaša's leader, became head of a German puppet state, the Independent State of Croatia (NDH), and established a one-party regime. The NDH moved against the more than one million Orthodox Serbs in Croatia, forcing some to convert and expelling or killing others in campaigns of genocide. About 250,000 Serbs in Croatia were eventually liquidated, many in village massacres. The regime also murdered some 40,000 Jews in concentration camps, such as the one at Jasenovac.

Elsewhere in Europe and in South Africa, Latin America, and the United States, fascist movements were racist, and sometimes specifically anti-Semitic, to varying degrees. In Poland members of the Falanga attacked Jews in the streets and created "ghetto benches" for Jewish students in the lecture rooms of the University of Warsaw. In the United States, the Ku Klux Klan and other groups preached the supremacy of the white race. Some fascists in Japan taught that the Japanese were a superior race, and Syrian fascists claimed superiority for their people as well.

Ku Klux Klan

The Ku Klux Klan (KKK) refers to either of two racist terrorist organizations in the United States.

The first was organized by veterans of the Confederate Army, first as a social club and then as a secret means of resisting Reconstruction and restoring white domination over newly enfranchised blacks. They apparently derived the name from the Greek word *kyklos*, from which comes the English "circle"; "Klan" was added for the sake of alliteration and Ku Klux Klan emerged. Dressed in white robes and sheets, Klansmen whipped and killed freedmen and their white supporters in nighttime raids. It had largely accomplished its goals by the 1870s before gradually fading away.

The second KKK arose in 1915, partly out of nostalgia for the Old South and partly out of fear of the rise of communism in Russia and the changing ethnic character of U.S. society. It counted Catholics, Jews, foreigners, and labour unions among its enemies. A burning cross became the symbol of the new organization, and white-robed Klansmen participated in marches, parades, and nighttime cross burnings all over the country. Its membership peaked in the 1920s at more than

Ku Klux Klan meeting, 1920s. Library of Congress, Washington, D.C.

four million, but during the Great Depression the organization gradually declined.

It became active again during the civil rights movement of the 1960s, attacking blacks and white civil rights workers with bombings, whippings, and shootings. By the end of the 20th century, growing racial tolerance had reduced its numbers to a few thousand. The Klan became a chronically fragmented mélange made up of several separate and competing groups, some of which occasionally entered into alliances with neo-Nazi and other right-wing extremist groups.

In contrast to fascists in most other European countries, Mussolini opposed anti-Semitism during the first 12 years of his rule. After 1933, however, he sometimes allowed anti-Semites within his party to condemn "unpatriotic" Jews in the press. In 1938 the Italian government passed anti-Semitic legislation, and later it abetted the Holocaust. Prior to the German takeover of Austria, the fascist regimes of Dollfuss and Schuschnigg also rejected anti-Semitism, and many Austrian Jews—including Sigmund Freud—supported them for resisting Nazism.

During the early interwar period, France's largest fascist parties—the Faisceau, the Young Patriots, the Cross of Fire, and the French Popular Party—rejected anti-Semitism, and right-wing Jews were accepted into these movements until at least 1936, when the left-wing Popular Front, under the premiership of the Jewish socialist Léon Blum, came to power. Other fascist groups, such as French Action and French Solidarity, were more openly anti-Semitic, though they claimed to object to Jews on "cultural" rather than racial grounds. In 1941 La Rocque placed responsibility for the "mortal vices" of France on Jews and Freemasons. Although British fascism was not anti-Semitic at the outset—Mosley's Blackshirts were trained by the British boxer Ted ("Kid") Lewis, who was Jewish—it became so by 1936.

Identification with Christianity

Most fascist movements portrayed themselves as defenders of Christianity and the traditional Christian family against atheists and amoral humanists. This was true of Catholic fascist movements in Poland, Spain, Portugal, France, Austria, Hungary, Croatia, Bolivia, Argentina, Chile, and Brazil. In Romania, Codreanu said he wanted to model his life after the crucified Christ of the Orthodox Church, and his Legion of the Archangel Michael, a forerunner of the Iron Guard, officially called for "faith in God" and "love for each other."

In France, Valois, Taittinger, Renaud, Bucard, and La Rocque were all Catholics, and Doriot, previously an atheist, appealed to Catholic sentiments after he became a fascist. Although Maurras was an agnostic, he defended the Catholic Church as a pillar of social order, and there were many Catholics among his followers. The fascist intellectual Robert Brasillach described the Spanish Civil War as a conflict between Catholic fascism and atheistic Marxism. Drieu La Rochelle rejected liberal Catholicism but praised the "virile, male Catholicism" of the Middle Ages and the "warrior Christianity of the Crusades."

Although fascists in Germany and Italy also posed as protectors of the church, their ideologies contained many elements that conflicted with traditional Christian beliefs, and their policies were sometimes opposed by church leaders. The Nazis criticized the Christian ideals of meekness and guilt on the grounds that they repressed the violent instincts necessary to prevent inferior races from dominating Aryans. Martin Bormann, the second most powerful official in the Nazi Party after 1941, argued that Nazi and Christian beliefs were "incompatible," primarily because the essential elements of Christianity were "taken over from Judaism." Bormann's views were shared by Hitler, who ultimately wished to replace Christianity with a racist form of warrior paganism. Although Hitler was cautious about dangerously alienating Christians during World War II, he sometimes permitted Nazi officials to put pressure on Protestant and Catholic parents to remove their children from religious classes and to register them for ideological instruction instead. In the Nazi schools charged with training Germany's future elite, Christian prayers were replaced with Teutonic rituals and sun-worship ceremonies.

Despite the many anti-Christian elements in Nazism, the vast majority of Nazis considered themselves to be religious, and most German anti-Semites supported Christianity purged of its "Jewish" elements. The pro-Nazi German Christians, who were part of the Lutheran Church in Germany, held that Christ had been a blond-haired, blue-eyed Aryan, and male members called themselves "SS men for Christ." In many German families children began their prayers before meals with the phrase, "Führer, my Führer, bequeathed to me by the Lord."

In Italy, Mussolini signed a concordat with the papacy, the Lateran Treaty (1929), which, among other things, made Roman Catholicism the state religion of Italy and mandated the teaching of Catholic doctrine in all public primary and secondary schools. Later, many practicing Catholics joined the conservative wing of the Fascist Party. In 1931, however, Pope Pius XI issued an encyclical, *Non abbiamo bisogno*, that denounced fascism's "pagan worship of the State" and its "revolution which snatches the young from the Church and from Jesus Christ, and which inculcates in its own young people hatred, violence and irreverence." Although many Italian fascists remained Catholic, the regime's mystique contained pagan elements that glorified the spirit of ancient Rome and the military virtues of its soldiers.

Support for Germany

Many non-German fascists were just as nationalistic toward their countries as Hitler was toward his. Many Polish fascists fell resisting the German invasion of 1939, and others were later condemned to Nazi concentration camps—as were some Hungarian fascists after 1942. Before he was assassinated in 1934, the Austrian fascist Dollfuss sought Mussolini's support against Hitler, and the Heimwehr

Members of the Heimwehr marching in Poland. The Heimwehr formed in Austria as a nationalistic group after World War I. Popperfoto/Getty Images

received important financial support from Mussolini to create a fascist government in Austria that would resist the Germans.

Before 1940 all French fascists opposed a German invasion of France. Doriot enlisted in the French army when war broke out between France and Germany in 1939, and in 1940, as a sergeant, he commanded a unit that held back the enemy for several hours (he was later decorated for his exploits). Following France's military defeat, some French fascists, including Doriot, subordinated their nationalism to Hitler's crusade against bolshevism, as did many Hungarian, Croatian, and other non-German fascists. Others, such as Philippe Barrès, a former member of the Faisceau, crossed the channel in 1940 to serve under Charles de Gaulle, leader of the Free French movement. Eugène Deloncle, one of the leaders of the Cagoule, France's major right-wing terrorist organization of the 1930s, was killed in 1944 while shooting at Gestapo agents who had come to arrest him. Another Cagoulard, François Duclos, was awarded the Croix de Guerre for his heroism in the Resistance. Salazar's Portugal and Franco's Spain remained officially neutral or nonbelligerent during World War II, despite the fascist characteristics of their own regimes.

Fascist Italy and fascist Japan were allies of Germany during the war, though Mussolini's autonomy in this alliance was lost when German divisions occupied Italy in 1942 following the landing of American and British troops in North Africa. In the mid-1930s, other non-German fascists, including members of the British Union of Fascists and the German-American Bund, expressed admiration for Hitler's forceful leadership without inviting a German invasion of their countries. Indeed, in 1938 La Rocque suggested that the best way for France to avoid such an invasion was to become more fascist itself. In 1941, following France's defeat by Hitler's armies, La Rocque called for "continental collaboration" with Germany and criticized de Gaulle and his British allies for threatening to "enslave" France. He soon became disillusioned with Germany's treatment of France, however, and in early 1942 he formed a resistance organization that provided military information to the British.

Intellectual Origins

Mussolini and Hitler did not invent fascist ideology. Indeed, fascism was neither a 20th-century creation nor a peculiarly Italian or German one. Originating in the 19th century, fascist ideas appeared in the works of writers from France as well as Austria, Germany, and Italy, including political theorists such as Theodor Fritsch, Paul Anton de Lagarde, Julius Langbehn, Jörg Lanz von Liebenfels, Joseph de Maistre, Charles Maurras, and Georges Sorel; scientists and philosophers such as Johann Gottlieb Fichte, Giovanni Gentile, Gustave Le Bon, Friedrich Nietzsche, Vilfredo Pareto, Karl Vogt, and Ernst Haeckel; historians and social thinkers such as Joseph-Arthur, comte de Gobineau, Hippolyte Taine, and Heinrich von Treitschke; artists, writers, and journalists such as Gabriele D'Annunzio, Richard Wagner, Édouard Drumont, Maurice Barrès, and Guido von List; and conservative politicians such as Otto Böckel and Adolf Stoecker.

Joseph de Maistre

Joseph de Maistre (b. April 1, 1753, Chambéry, France–d. Feb. 26, 1821, Turin, kingdom of Sardinia [Italy]) was a French polemical author, moralist, and diplomat who, after being uprooted by the French Revolution in 1789, became a great exponent of the conservative tradition.

Maistre studied with the Jesuits and became a member of the Savoy Senate in 1787, following the civil career of his father, a former Senate president. After the invasion of Savoy by the armies of Napoleon in 1792, he began his lifelong exile in Switzerland, where he frequented the literary salon of Germaine de Staël in Coppet. Appointed envoy to St. Petersburg by the king of Sardinia in 1803, he remained at the Russian court for 14 years, writing *Essay on the Generative Principle of Political Constitutions* (1814) and his best work (unfinished), *The St. Petersburg Dialogues* (1821). On his recall he settled in Turin as chief magistrate and minister of state of the Sardinian kingdom.

Maistre was convinced of the need for the supremacy of Christianity and the absolute rule of both sovereign and pope. He also insisted on the necessity of the public executioner as a negative guardian of social order, writing in *The St. Petersburg Dialogues* that "all power, all subordination rests on the *(continued on the next page)*

(continued on the next page)

executioner: he is the horror and the bond of human association. Remove this incomprehensible agent from the world,
and the very moment order gives way to chaos, thrones
topple, and society disappears." A devoutly religious
Roman Catholic, he explained both the French Revolution and the French revolutionary and Napoleonic wars as
religious expiation for the sins of the times. He opposed
the progress of science and the liberal beliefs and empirical
methods of philosophers such as Francis Bacon (1561–1626),
Voltaire (1694–1778), Jean-Jacques
Rousseau (1712–78), and John
Locke (1632–1704). He also
wrote *On the Pope* (1819)
and *Letters on the Spanish
Inquisition* (1838), an apology for the punitive role
of the Spanish Inqui-
sition. In both works
Maistre defended
absolutism with rig-
orous logic, and it
was as a logical think-
er, pursuing con-
sequences from an
accepted premise,
that Maistre excelled.
The French poet
Charles Baudelaire
(1821–67) acknowledged
that it was Maistre who
taught him to think.

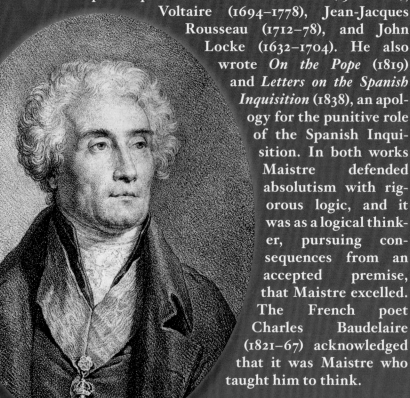

Joseph de Maistre, engraving. Giraudon/Art Resource, New York

Many fascist ideas derived from the reactionary backlash to the progressive revolutions of 1789, 1830, 1848, and 1871 and to the secular liberalism and social radicalism that accompanied these upheavals. De Maistre condemned the 18th-century Enlightenment for having subverted the dominance of traditional religion and traditional elites and paid homage to the public executioner as the protector of a divinely sanctioned social hierarchy. Taine lamented the rise to power of the masses, whom he suggested were at a lower stage of biological evolution than aristocrats. Le Bon wrote a primer on how to divert the barbarism of the masses from revolution to reaction. Barrès fused ethnic rootedness with authoritarian nationalism and contended that too much civilization led to decadence and that hatred and violence were energizing remedies.

German populist politicians and writers such as Stoecker, Böckel, and Fritsch extolled the idea of racially pure peasants close to the soil who would one day follow a charismatic leader able to intuit the *Volk* soul without benefit of elections. Anti-Semitism was a staple in the work of Drumont, Maurras, Lagarde, Langbehn, and a host of other best-selling authors. Britain's Houston Stewart Chamberlain preached Aryan racism, and many of the anti-Semitic ideas espoused by Carl Lueger's Christian Social Party and Georg von Schönerer's Pan-German movement in Austria were later adopted by Hitler.

Racial Darwinists such as Vogt, Haeckel, Treitschke, Langbehn, Lagarde, and Chamberlain glorified the survival of the fittest, scolded humanitarians for attempting to protect the racially unfit, and rejected the idea of social equality ("Equality is death, hierarchy is life," wrote Langbehn). Chamberlain saw no reason to give inferior races equal rights. Treitschke raged against democracy, socialism, and feminism (all of which he attributed to Jews), insisted that might made right, and praised warrior imperialism ("Brave peoples expand, cowardly peoples perish"). Lagarde said of the Slavs that "the sooner they perish the better it will be for us and them," and he called for the extermination of the Jews—a sentiment that was shared by his contemporary Langbehn. As John Weiss remarked of Lagarde and Langbehn, "The two most influential and popular intellectuals of late nineteenth century Germany were indistinguishable from Nazi ideologists." Weiss also noted that "the press and popular magazines of Germany and Central Europe had fed a steady diet of racial nationalism to the public since the last quarter of the nineteenth century, and anti-Semitic stereotypes were nothing if not commonplace in German mass culture."

In the late 19th century many conservative nationalists were philosophical idealists who accused liberals and socialists of materialism and thereby portrayed their own politics as more spiritual. Other 19th-century thinkers propagated some protofascist ideas while rejecting others. Nietzsche rhapsodized about the heroic vitality of elite souls who were uninhibited by Christian ethics or liberal humanitarianism, but he was appalled by *völkisch* nationalism and anti-Semitism. Similarly, Sorel preached violence as an antidote for decadence—an idea that Mussolini admired—but his economic thought was too socialistic for most fascists.

Social Bases of Fascist Movements

Despite their long history in European thought, fascist ideas prospered politically only when perceived economic threats increased their appeal to members of certain social groups. In 1928, before the onset of the Great Depression in Germany, Hitler received less than 3 percent of the vote; after 1930, however, far more voters—many of them middle and lower-middle-class individuals fearful of "proletarianization"—gave him their support. The economic anxiety underlying the success of Nazism was reflected to some extent in party membership, which was drawn disproportionately from economic elites and other high-status groups—especially for leadership positions. These posts also contained large numbers of university professors, high school teachers, higher civil servants, former military officers, doctors, lawyers, businessmen, and landed aristocrats. In the lower ranks of the party, white-collar workers were overrepresented and blue-collar workers were underrepresented. Similarly, in Italy, as historian Charles Maier has shown, fascism originally received most of its support from large and small landowners who felt beleaguered by landless farm workers and from businessmen and white-collar workers who felt a similar threat from industrial workers. In 1927, 75 percent of the membership of Mussolini's party came from the middle and lower-middle classes and only 15 percent from the working class. Nearly 10 percent came from Italy's economic elites, who represented a much smaller portion of the general population.

The Nazis drew more support from small towns than they did from large cities. In rural areas, Protestants were overrepresented in the party, and Catholics were underrepresented. In less-industrialized countries—such as Spain, Portugal, Poland, Romania, and Hungary—fascists relied more heavily on rural support. In Japan many fascist activists were originally young army officers, low-level civil servants, small landowners, small factory owners, masters of small workshops, primary school teachers, and Shinto and Buddhist priests.

Fascism and Nonfascist Conservatisms: Collaboration and Crossover

Although in principle there were significant differences between fascism and nonfascist conservatism, the two camps shared some of the same goals, which in times of crisis led some nonfascists to collaborate with fascists. As Weiss observed, "Any study of fascism which centers too narrowly on the fascists and Nazis alone may miss the true significance of right-wing extremism. For without necessarily becoming party members or accepting the entire range of party principles themselves, aristocratic landlords, army officers, government and civil service officials, and important industrialists in Italy and Germany helped bring fascists to power." Without the aid of President Paul von Hindenburg, Chancellor Franz von Papen, and other German conservatives, Hitler, who never won an electoral majority, would not have been appointed chancellor.

During the Great Depression, thousands of middle-class conservatives fearful of the growing power of the left abandoned traditional right-wing parties and adopted fascism. The ideological distance travelled from traditional conservatism to Nazism was sometimes small, since many of the ideas that Hitler exploited in the 1930s had long been common currency within the German right.

In Italy thousands of landowners and businessmen were grateful to Mussolini's Blackshirts for curbing the socialists in 1920–21, and many in the army and the Catholic Church saw fascism as a bulwark against communism. Before the beginning of Franco's rule in Spain, many monarchists had close relations with the Falange. Although the Franco regime arrested some of its fascist rivals, it gave others important positions in its propaganda agencies. Horthy's government

From left to right, Franz von Papen, Adolf Hitler, Hermann Göring, and Wilhelm
Frick on Germany's National Day of Mourning, 1933. Although Papen did not
identify as a Nazi, he was instrumental in Hitler's rise to power. Keystone-France/
Gamma-Keystone/Getty Images

in Hungary was soft on fascism, and in its early stages it
employed fascist methods itself, sending strong-arm squads
to raid leftist trade unions, clubs, and newspaper offices and
countenancing the slaughter of hundreds of communists and
socialists throughout the country. In Greece, King George II
and conservatives in the parliament helped Metaxas to establish his dictatorship in 1936.

Fascists also received support from Christian conservatives. Between 1930 and 1932 Hitler was supported by many
Protestant voters in rural Prussia, and after 1933 the Catholic Church in Germany largely accommodated itself to his
regime. In 1933 the Vatican, which had previously interdicted
Catholic membership in socialist organizations, signed a concordat with Germany that forbade priests to speak out on
politics and gave Hitler a say in naming bishops.

In France the leading Catholic newspaper, *La Croix*, expressed early support for Hitler's crusade against bolshevism, and the largest Catholic parliamentary party, the Republican Federation (Fédération Republicaine), included fascists in its ranks. In 1936, when the Cross of Fire became an electoral party (changing its name to the French Social Party), it absorbed much of the Republican Federation's membership.

CHAPTER 4

NEOFASCISM AROUND THE WORLD

Although fascism was largely discredited in Europe at the end of World War II, fascist-inspired movements were founded in several European countries beginning in the late 1940s. Similar groups were created outside Europe as well, primarily in Latin America, the Middle East, and South Africa. Like their fascist predecessors, the "neofascists" advocated militant nationalism and authoritarian values, opposed the liberal individualism of the Enlightenment, attacked Marxist and other left-wing ideologies, indulged in racist and xenophobic scapegoating, portrayed themselves as protectors of traditional national culture and religion, glorified violence and military heroism, and promoted populist right-wing economic programs.

Despite these similarities, however, neofascism was not simply a revival of fascism. Neofascist parties differed from earlier fascist movements in several significant respects, many of them having to do with the profound political, economic, and social changes that took place in Europe in the first decades after the end of the war. For example, whereas fascists assigned much of the blame for their countries' economic problems to the machinations of bolsheviks, liberals, and Jews, neofascists tended to focus on non-European immigrants—such as Turks, Pakistanis, and Algerians—who arrived in increasing numbers beginning in the 1970s.

After decades of postwar decolonization, neofascists in Western Europe lost interest in taking *Lebensraum* through military conquest of other states. Instead, they fought battles for "urban space," which in Germany involved conflicts over government-subsidized housing for immigrants. With increasing urbanization also came a shift in the electoral bases of fascist-oriented movements and a consequent decline in the importance of rural romanticism ("blood and soil") in neofascist political rhetoric. Finally, the gradual acceptance of democratic norms by the vast majority of Western Europeans reduced the appeal of authoritarian ideologies and required that neofascist parties make a concerted effort to portray themselves as democratic and "mainstream." Some neofascists even included words like "democratic" and "liberal" in the titles of their movements. Most neofascists abandoned the outward trappings of earlier fascist parties, such as paramilitary uniforms and Roman salutes, and many explicitly denounced fascist policies or denied that their parties were fascist. Noting this transformation, in 1996 Roger Eatwell cautioned: "Beware of men—and women—wearing smart Italian suits: the colour is now gray, the material is cut to fit the times, but the aim is still power....Fascism is on the move once more, even if its most sophisticated forms have learned to dress to suit the times." Similarly, historian Richard Wolin described these movements as "designer fascism."

As with fascist movements of the interwar period, neofascist movements differed from one another in various respects. The rhetoric of neofascists in Russia and the Balkans, for example, tended to be more openly brutal and militaristic than that of the majority of their Western counterparts. Most neofascist movements in Europe pandered to anti-Semitism, though neofascists in Italy and Spain generally did not. Spanish neofascists also differed from most other neofascists in Europe in that they did not make a major issue of immigration. Portuguese,

British, and (for a time) Italian neofascists advocated corporatism, in contrast to French and many other Western neofascists, who promoted free-market capitalism and lower taxes. In the 1990s in Russia and Eastern Europe, neofascist movements were generally more leftist than their counterparts in Western Europe, emphasizing the interests of workers and peasants over those of the urban middle class and calling for "mixed" socialist and capitalist economies.

Italy

One of the largest neofascist movements in Western Europe in the 1990s was the Italian Social Movement (Movimento Sociale Italiano [MSI]; renamed the National Alliance [Alleanza Nazionale] in 1994). Founded in 1946, it was led at various times by Giorgio Almirante, Augusto De Marsanich, Arturo Michelini, and Gianfranco Fini. As an official in Mussolini's Italian Social Republic, a puppet state established by the Germans in northern Italy in 1944, Almirante oversaw the regime's propaganda machinery. When the MSI was launched in 1946, Almirante sought to give it a modern image, urging its members to "beware of

Italian politician Gianfranco Fini, formerly a leader of the National Alliance. ISM Agency/Getty Images

representing fascism in a grotesque way, or at any rate, in an outdated, anachronistic, and stupidly nostalgic way."

Although Italy's postwar constitution forbade the reorganization of a fascist party, and although Almirante discouraged MSI members from wearing paramilitary black shirts and performing the Roman salute, the propaganda of the MSI echoed a number of themes identified with interwar fascism. First and foremost was its call for the "vital forces" of the nation to resist the communist menace. The MSI contended that not only were communists gaining footholds in the press, in the schools, among intellectuals, and in the trade unions, but they were behind the breakdown of law and order and left-wing terrorism. In the 1950s MSI members entered schools to assault leftists and provoked violent confrontations with socialist and communist activists during election campaigns and strikes.

The MSI extolled the virtues of virility, courage, action, and patriotism. Like the National Fascist Party before it, the MSI also called for a corporatist solution to class conflict and the subordination of individual interests to the good of the nation. As a defender of "Christian civilization," it supported the Lateran Treaty, which made Roman Catholicism the state religion of Italy (Catholicism ceased to be the official religion with the signing of the concordat of 1984), and the legal prohibition of divorce.

Although at times the MSI cultivated a benign image and obscured its fascist imagery, at other times it called attention to its continuity with the fascist past. The practice of avoiding direct references to fascism virtually disappeared from MSI propaganda in the 1980s and '90s, as illustrated by the declaration of Fini, elected party secretary in 1987: "Fascism was part of the history of Italy and the expression of permanent values." At a campaign rally in October 1992, Alessandra Mussolini, the granddaughter of the duce, stood in the balcony of the 15th-century Palazzo Venezia (Venice Palace) shouting, *"Grazie nonno!"* ("Thanks, Granddad!") as thousands of MSI supporters, many wearing black shirts and giving the fascist salute, marched below her and chanted, "Duce! Duce!"

MSI electoral fortunes varied greatly according to circumstances, ranging from about 2 percent of the vote in 1948 to 13.5 percent in 1994. In local elections in 1993, Fini and Mussolini were nearly elected mayor of Rome and mayor of Naples, respectively, and the party won almost a third of the vote in both cities.

Immediately after these elections, Fini subsumed the MSI into a new and allegedly more respectable party, the National Alliance (AN). Officially rejecting "any form of dictatorship or totalitarianism," he replaced the old slogan of a "third way" between capitalism and communism with praise for the free market and individual initiative. In March 1995 the AN won about 14 percent of the vote and five ministerial posts in a coalition government led by Silvio Berlusconi. Later that year the AN led an attempt to repeal the clause in the Italian constitution forbidding the reorganization of a fascist party, but the effort failed. Although Fini described the AN as "postfascist," following the 1994 elections, he declared that Mussolini was the greatest Italian statesman of the 20th century and that fascism before 1938—i.e., before Mussolini formed a military alliance with Hitler—was "mostly good."

Germany

In 1949 Fritz Dorls and Otto Ernst Remer, a former army general who had helped to crush an attempted military coup against Hitler in July 1944, founded the Socialist Reich Party (Sozialistische Reichspartei; SRP), one of the earliest neofascist parties in Germany. Openly sympathetic to Nazism, the SRP made considerable gains in former Nazi strongholds, and in 1951 it won 11 percent of the vote in regional elections in Lower Saxony. The party was banned as a neo-Nazi organization in 1952.

Among legal neofascist parties in Germany, the most important were the National Democratic Party of Germany (Nationaldemokratische Partei Deutschlands; NPD), founded in 1964 by Waldemar Schütz, a former member of the Nazi Party and the Waffen-SS (the elite military wing of the Nazi Party, which served in combat alongside the regular German army); the German People's Union (Deutsche Volksunion; DVU), founded in 1971; and the Republicans (Die Republikaner; REP), founded in 1983 by another former Waffen-SS member, Franz Schönhuber. Like Almirante in Italy, Schönhuber strove to give his party a more respectable image, and his efforts extended to denying his own previous connection with the Waffen-SS. "I have no Nazi past," he said. "I regard the National Socialist state as absolutely incompatible with the rule of law. Racism and fascism led us into the most horrible catastrophe in our national history."

Neofascist parties in Germany focused much of their energies on campaigns against immigrants, and they were most successful in areas where immigrant communities were large. Running on slogans such as "Germany for the Germans, the boat is full," the REP gained 7.5 percent of the vote in West German elections in 1989 and more than 7 percent of the vote in elections for the European Parliament in the same year. Neofascist parties also won significant support among disaffected youth in parts of the former East Germany, where there were high levels of unemployment, poor housing, and severe environmental problems in the years immediately following unification.

In 1992–93 gangs of neo-Nazi youth in eastern Germany, most of whom did not belong to political parties, staged attacks on Turkish and other immigrants and desecrated Jewish cemeteries. Public revulsion at the attacks contributed to a temporary dip in the far-right vote in 1993. At the end of the 1990s, the REP was torn by personal, generational, and tactical divisions, with some members favouring a blatantly pro-Nazi platform and others urging more moderate and mainstream positions.

Austria

In 1999–2000 a series of electoral successes by the far-right Freedom Party of Austria (Freiheitlichen Partei Österreichs; FPÖ), founded in 1956 and led from 1986 by Jörg Haider, created a storm of controversy and produced widespread protests in Austria and abroad, largely because of perceptions that the leadership of the party, including Haider himself, was sympathetic to Nazism. Haider, whose father had been a leading member of the Austrian Nazi Party before and during World War II, became notorious for his praise of Hitler's employment policies and his remark, made to a group of Austrian veterans of World War II, that the Waffen-SS deserved "honour and respect." Arguing for stricter controls on immigration, he warned against the "over-foreignization" of Austrian society, pointedly borrowing a term—*Überfremdung*—used by Joseph Goebbels, Hitler's minister of propaganda.

Jörg Haider

Jörg Haider (b. Jan. 26, 1950, Bad Goisern, Austria–d. Oct. 11, 2008, near Klagenfurt) was a controversial Austrian politician who served as leader of the far-right Freedom Party of Austria (1986–2000) and Alliance for the Future of Austria (2005–08) and as governor of the *Bundesland* (federal state) of Kärnten (1989–91; 1999–2008).

(continued on the next page)

Haider studied at the University of Vienna, where he received a law degree in 1973 and subsequently taught law. As a student, he became chairman of the youth organization of the Freedom Party of Austria (Freiheitliche Partei Öster-reichs; FPÖ). He later was elected secretary of the party in Kärnten (Carinthia). In 1979, at age 29, he was elected to the national parliament. In 1983 Haider was chosen to be chairman of the FPÖ in Kärnten; in 1986 he became chairman of the federal party. The charismatic Haider transformed the party, increasing its popular appeal. Prior to his leadership, it had performed poorly, while the country's two main parties,

Jörg Haider. Northfoto/Shutterstock.com

the Social Democratic Party of Austria (Sozialdemokratische Partei Österreichs; SPÖ) and the conservative Austrian People's Party (Österreichische Volkspartei; ÖVP), had dominated at both state and federal levels. Following state elections in 1989, however, the FPÖ finished second to the SPÖ and formed a coalition with the ÖVP, enabling Haider's election as governor of Kärnten. But in 1991, partly as a result of Haider's praise for the employment policies of Adolf Hitler, the coalition dissolved, and he was forced to resign.

Nevertheless, under Haider's leadership, the FPÖ had a virtually unbroken string of successes in increasing its strength at all levels, as well as in elections for the European Parliament. Some observers attributed a measure of his support to the Austrian people's disgust with their government, which had become an entrenched bureaucracy known for mismanagement and for a succession of scandals. Haider virulently denounced immigration and opposed the expansion of the European Union (EU) to the east—positions that were applauded by a wide spectrum of Austrians. Moreover, he was charismatic and a skillful orator. Yet many observers expressed alarm that the sentiments to which he gave voice could find such a large audience in Austria. Particularly controversial were the number of statements he made about Hitler and the Nazis. In a speech in 1995, for example, he defended and praised members of the Waffen-SS, calling them "decent people of good character." He also described Nazi concentration camps as "punishment camps." Still, he maintained that he was not anti-Semitic and that he deplored the Holocaust.

Haider was reelected governor of Kärnten in March 1999, when the FPÖ won the state elections with 42 percent of the vote. In the national parliamentary elections held that October, the FPÖ registered its strongest showing to date; garnering 27 percent of the national vote, it overtook the ÖVP for second place. Its success threatened the national coalition of the ÖVP and the SPÖ. After months of unsuccessful negotiations with the SPÖ, the ÖVP unexpectedly formed a coalition government

(continued on the next page)

with the FPÖ. This development sparked protests throughout Vienna and in the international community; it prompted the Israeli government to recall its ambassador, and the EU imposed political sanctions against the country. Haider was forced to resign as leader of the FPÖ, though he remained active in the party and continued as governor of Kärnten. Despite the FPÖ's poor showing in the 2002 national elections, Haider was reelected governor in 2004. His final split with the FPÖ occurred when he announced he was forming a new party, the Alliance for the Future of Austria (Bündnis Zukunft Österreich; BZÖ), in 2005.

In the 2006 national elections the BZÖ won 4 percent of the vote, capturing seven seats. Two years later the party showed strong gains, garnering 11 percent, and Haider seemed poised for a comeback on the national stage. On Oct. 11, 2008, however, he died from injuries sustained in a car accident.

Haider became governor of Carinthia, his home province, in March 1999, when the FPÖ won regional elections there with 42 percent of the vote. In general elections in October, the FPÖ narrowly outpolled the conservative Austrian People's Party (Österreichische Volkspartei; ÖVP) with 27 percent of the vote and thereby became the second largest party in Austria (the Social-Democratic Party of Austria [Sozialdemokratische Partei Österreichs; SPÖ] finished first, with more than 33 percent). The prospect that the FPÖ would be included in a new Austrian government prompted a threat by the other member states of the European Union (EU) to suspend all bilateral political contacts with Austria. Despite the warning, the ÖVP, with considerable reluctance, formed a government with the FPÖ in February 2000, granting the party five cabinet ministries (Haider himself was not given a cabinet post).

The new government was greeted by widespread demon-strations, diplomatic protests, and calls for boycotts on travel to Austrian tourist destinations. Facing intense international pressure, Haider resigned his leadership of the FPÖ at the end of February, only three weeks after his party had entered the government. In 2005, he announced that he was forming a new party, the Alliance for the Future of Austria (Bündnis Zuku-nft Österreich; BZÖ), marking his final split with the FPÖ. Although the new party made gains in 2008, Haider died on Oct. 11 of that year before he could make a national comeback.

France

In the late 20th and early 21st centuries, neofascism in France was dominated by the National Front (Front National; FN), founded in 1972 by François Duprat and François Brigneau and led beginning later that year by Jean-Marie Le Pen. After 10 years on the margins of French politics, the FN began a period of spectacular growth in 1981. Campaigning on the slogan "France for the French" (as had French fascists in the 1930s) and linking high unemployment and increased crime to the presence of immigrants, the FN increased its support from 1 percent of the vote in 1981 to 14 percent in 1988. In 1984 the FN gained 11 percent of the vote in elections for the European Parliament and thereby became the largest extreme-right group within that body. In municipal elections in 1989 the FN won city council seats in more than one third of cities exceeding 20,000 inhabitants, and in 1995–97 it gained control of four southern cities—Marignane, Orange, Toulon, and Vitrolles. Le Pen won 15 percent of the vote in presidential elections in 1995, and the FN also took 15 per-cent in legislative elections in May–June 1997. In areas of its greatest strength—southern and eastern France—the FN won more than 20 percent.

Jean-Marie Le Pen

Jean-Marie Le Pen (b. June 20, 1928, La Trinité, France) is a French nationalist who founded and served as leader (1972–2011) of the National Front political party, which represented the main right-wing opposition to the country's mainstream conservative parties from the 1970s through the early 21st century. A controversial figure who frequently was a presidential candidate, Le Pen was accused by his opponents of xenophobia and anti-Semitism.

Le Pen, the son of a sailor, was born in a coastal village in Brittany and attended a Jesuit boarding school in Vannes. In the 1940s he attended law school at the University of Paris and

Jean-Marie Le Pen speaking at a rally. Thomas Samson/Gamma-Rapho/ Getty Images

in 1954 joined the French Foreign Legion, serving as a para-trooper in Algeria and in French Indochina. Upon his return to France, Le Pen became a follower of publisher Pierre Poujade, who was then leading an anti-taxation protest movement, and in 1956 he was elected to the National Assembly (parliament) as its youngest deputy. Reelected to the National Assembly in 1958, he was defeated in 1962, after which he founded a society that sold recordings of Nazi speeches and German military songs.

In 1972 Le Pen formed the National Front political party. From the outset Le Pen's party stressed the threat to France posed by immigration—particularly of Arab immigration from France's former colonies in North Africa. The party also opposed European integration, favoured the reintroduction of capital punishment, and sought prohibitions on the building of additional mosques in France. Le Pen himself was constantly embroiled in political controversy; for example, in the 1960s he was given a two-month suspended prison sentence and fined 10,000 francs for an "apology of war crimes"; he was found guilty of violating France's law prohibiting Holocaust denial for com-ments made in the 1980s describing the Holocaust as a mere "detail" in the history of World War II; and in 1998 he was con-victed of assaulting a political opponent and was banned from holding or seeking office for two years.

Nevertheless, Le Pen's style and policies captured sig-nificant support, particularly from the working class, which suffered from rising crime and high unemployment during the 1980s and '90s. He ran several times for the presidency; though he captured less than 1 percent in 1974, in 1988 and 1995 he won some 15 percent. In 2002 Le Pen defeated Prime Minister Lionel Jospin in the first round of the presidential election, winning 18 percent of the vote. However, with nearly the entire French political establishment—including the Socialist Party and the French Communist Party—endorsing conservative President Jacques Chirac and with mass demon-strations against Le Pen throughout the country, he was eas-ily defeated in the second round. In 2007 he garnered slightly

(continued on the next page)

more than 10 percent of the vote in the first round, which was insufficient to qualify him for the runoff. Three years later Le Pen announced that he would be retiring as National Front leader, and in January 2011 he was succeeded by his daughter Marine Le Pen.

From 1984 into the early 21st century, Le Pen served as an elected member of the European Parliament. In 2005 he strongly opposed the proposed constitution of the European Union, which French voters ultimately rejected. In May 2009 the European Parliament voted to prevent Le Pen from presiding over its opening session, to be held after the European elections in June; it did so by members overturning a rule that allowed the oldest member of the body—Le Pen, assuming his reelection—to address the new assembly.

The FN's rapid increase in popularity occurred despite Le Pen's previous association with extreme right-wing causes, his cavalier remarks about the Holocaust (in 1987 he told a television interviewer that the Holocaust was only "a detail of history"), the presence of former fascists in his organization, and other neofascist aspects of his movement.

The FN's popular anti-immigrant themes included the claim that non-French immigrants, especially Muslims, threatened French national identity and culture—a threat that had been compounded, according to the FN, by the huge influx of films, music, and television programs from the United States. The FN also called for a return to traditional values—family, law and order, hard work, and patriotism—and claimed that these values had been eroded by liberal permissiveness and multiculturalism.

Although Le Pen described himself as a "Churchillian democrat," his commitment to political democracy was similar to that of La Rocque in the 1930s and '40s—more tactical than principled. "We must be respectful of legality while it exists," he declared in 1982. Just as La Rocque had admired Mussolini, so Le Pen admired Franco in Spain and Augusto Pinochet in Chile. Le Pen praised Pinochet's overthrow of socialist president Salvador Allende in 1973, and he declared that the French army should follow Pinochet's example if a similar leftist government were to arise in France.

The FN attempted to portray Le Pen as a plain-speaking man of the people, and it emphasized his physical strength and virility. Although Le Pen's bodyguards sometimes wore helmets and battle gear similar to those of France's national riot police, and although party supporters were sometimes involved in street violence against immigrants and ethnic minorities, the FN had no official party uniforms or paramilitary organizations.

The FN imposed censorship when it had the power to do so. Mayors of cities governed by the FN removed left-wing journals from municipal libraries, forbade librarians to order "internationalist" books, and required the purchase of materials supporting the FN's views. The mayor of Toulon, Jean-Marie Le Chevallier, canceled the award of a literary prize to a Jewish writer and tried to shut down a well-known performance festival in the city because of its leftist political orientation.

The FN's positions on economic issues fluctuated during the 1980s and '90s. In the 1980s it sided with conservatives who stressed individual entrepreneurship and opposed state intervention in the economy. However, in 1993, in an attempt to attract more working-class voters, Le Pen described free-market economics as "harmful" unless balanced with state intervention, and he called for a 39-hour workweek, five weeks of paid vacation, and other social benefits—all measures the FN had previously opposed. In 1996 he reversed himself again, calling for lower taxes and criticizing trade unions for engaging in strikes.

By the 1990s the FN had acquired a broad-based and diverse following, including small-business owners and self-employed artisans, unemployed white-collar and blue-collar workers, socially conservative Catholics, and young people. In 1998 Le Pen's associate Bruno Mégret split from the FN to form a new party, the National Movement (Mouvement National; MN), taking with him most of the FN's departmental secretaries and city councillors. Nevertheless, Le Pen's style and policies continued to attract significant support, and he served as an elected member of the European Parliament well into the 21st century. In 2002 Le Pen defeated Prime Minister Lionel Jospin in the first round of the presidential election, winning 18 percent of the vote. However, with nearly the entire French political establishment—including the Socialist Party and the French Communist Party—endorsing conservative President Jacques Chirac, he was easily defeated in the second round.

Russia

After the end of World War II, few Russians needed to be reminded of the evils of German fascism. Nevertheless, several fascist groups emerged in Russia after the breakup of the Soviet Union in 1991. Resentment over the loss of the Soviet empire, concern for the fate of ethnic Russians in the successor states, bad economic conditions, the breakdown of law and order, the desire for a strong leader, and the fact that democratic institutions were not deeply rooted in Russia all combined to make fascist ideas appealing to some segments of the Russian population.

Some Russian fascists attempted to revive the reactionary ideology of the Black Hundreds, a loose association of extreme right-wing organizations formed in Russia during the early years of the 20th century. Black Hundred ideology was highly nationalistic, anticosmopolitan, anti-Semitic, anti-Masonic, anti-Western, antidemocratic, antiegalitarian, antiliberal, and anti-"decadence." The Black Hundreds were strong supporters of the Russian Orthodox Church, the army, and authoritarian government (favouring either monarchy or military dictatorship), and they indulged in conspiracy theories that blamed most of Russia's troubles on Jews and Freemasons.

In the 1980s the leading group espousing Black Hundred ideology was Pamyat ("Memory"), whose main spokesman after 1984 was Dmitry Vasiliev. During the communist era Pamyat worked for the restoration of churches and national monuments in Moscow, and Vasiliev generally supported the Communist Party and praised Lenin, Stalin, and the KGB for defending national traditions. After 1989, however, Vasiliev increasingly supported the Russian Orthodox Church and began to advocate monarchism. Pamyat writers denounced communists as "godless," "cosmopolitan," and "antipatriotic," and they criticized the neglect of national traditions, anti-Russian sentiment in the Baltic countries, the moral decline of youth, increased crime, the weakening of the family, and alcoholism. Although Pamyat had a near monopoly on the extreme right in 1987–88, by 1991 it had been overtaken by rival movements.

One of these movements was the Liberal-Democratic Party of Russia (Liberalno-Demokraticheskaya Partiya Rossi; LDPR), led by Vladimir Zhirinovsky. Founded in 1990, the party grew rapidly, and in presidential elections in 1991 Zhirinovsky won almost 8 percent of the vote, which placed him third after Boris Yeltsin and Nicolay Ryzhkov. In parliamentary elections in 1993, the LDPR gained nearly 23 percent of the vote, more than the Russian Communist Party (12.4

percent) did. However, by 1996 Zhirinovsky's support had declined precipitously, and in presidential elections that year he managed to win only 6 percent of the vote.

Most neofascists denied that they were "fascists," and Zhirinovsky was no exception. On various occasions he asserted his adherence to democratic values, the rights of man, a multiparty system, and the rule of law. However, in 1991 he declared: "I say quite plainly, when I come to power there will be a dictatorship. Russia needs a dictator now." He added: "I'll be ruthless. I will close down the newspapers one after another. I may have to shoot 100,000 people, but the other 300 million will live peacefully. You want to call it Russian fascism, fine."

Zhirinovsky also indulged in racism and anti-Semitism, even though his own father was apparently Jewish and he himself had been active in a Russian Jewish group in 1989. When asked about his parents in 1993, he replied, "My mother was Russian, my

Vladimir Zhirinovsky. © AP Images

father a lawyer"—a comment that became a popular joke in Russia about people who try to conceal their origins. Zhirinovsky also claimed that the Russian Revolution of 1917 was mainly the work of "baptized Jews" and that the state of Israel and Mossad, the Israeli intelligence agency, were engaged in anti-Russian conspiracies. Although he sometimes complained that the United States was becoming a nonwhite society, he declared that only an alliance between the United States, Germany, and Russia could "preserve the white race on the European and American continents."

Zhirinovsky wanted to ensure Russia's greatness by retaining control of the constituent republics of the former Soviet Union, and he condemned independence movements in the Baltic states and Chechnya and threatened harsh measures against them. As he told a Lithuanian newspaper in 1991, "I'll destroy you. I'll bury nuclear waste...along the border [with the Baltic states]....You Lithuanians will die from diseases and radiation.... Soon there will be no Lithuanians, Estonians, and Latvians in the Baltic. I'll act the way Hitler did in 1942." Zhirinovsky made similar threats to Western countries, which he believed were working against Russia's interests. On a visit to Belgrade in 1994, he warned the West to stay out of the conflict in the Balkans or risk a Russian nuclear attack. After being denied a visa to Germany in the same year, he threatened to completely destroy that country and occupy it with 300,000 Russian troops.

Like many fascists of the interwar period, Zhirinovsky had little regard for women, and he was openly contemptuous of women with education or political power. Following a television debate with a representative of the Women's Movement of Russia in 1995, he remarked that women such as her enjoyed being beaten and had fantasies about being raped, though they were too ugly for their fantasies to come true. Such comments were consistent with the negative portrayal of women—especially younger women—in Black Hundreds literature.

Zhirinovsky's economic program favoured a mixed economy. He proposed both that taxes on industry be reduced and that 70 percent of the economy be controlled by the state, including transportation and communication. However, he blamed most of Russia's economic problems on scapegoats, claiming that Russia was so poor because the country had been robbed of its natural resources by Jews, Freemasons, and Americans.

The Russian National Unity (Russkoe Natsionalnoe Edinstvo; RNE), a paramilitary organization founded in 1990 by Aleksandr Barkashov, claimed to have an extensive network of local branches, but its electoral support was significantly less than that of the LDPR. Barkashov, a former commando in the Russian army, touted his blackshirts as a reserve force for the Russian army and the Ministry of Internal Affairs. He blamed many of Russia's economic problems on Jews, claimed that two RNE blackshirts had been victims of Jewish ritual murder, insisted that only a "few hundred" Jews had perished in German concentration camps, and said that the Holocaust was a "diversion" created to conceal a Jewish-inspired genocide of 100 million Russians. The RNE's symbol was a left-pointed swastika together with a four-pointed star. The RNE emphasized the "primary importance" of Russian blood, accused "internationalists-communists" of undermining the "genetic purity" of the nation with a program of racial mixture, and called for a rebirth of "Russian-Aryan traditions." Although Barkashov denied that he was a fascist, he admired Hitler enormously, once stating that "I consider [Hitler] a great hero of the German nation and of all white races. He succeeded in inspiring the entire nation to fight against degradation and the washing away of national values."

Barkashov insisted in 1994 that he would come to power by "absolutely legal means." Nevertheless, the RNE's program stated that conventional democracy was inefficient, and it called for an "ethnic democracy" in which the right to vote would be restricted to those who had demonstrated their loyalty to the nation. As part of Barkashov's program of racist nationalism, he insisted that the state should protect motherhood to ensure the growth of the ethnic Russian population. Families with many children should be rewarded, and a "cult of the family" should be encouraged on a "traditional patriarchal basis." Farmers, he said, were the best part of the nation, representing as they did a union of blood and soil. A major plank in the RNE's platform was its defense of ethnic Russians outside Russia proper. Barkashov denounced the oppression of ethnic Russians in Estonia and Latvia and later supported Russian military intervention in Chechnya to protect Russian citizens "from force and arbitrary rule," calling for harsh measures—ranging from temporary internment to deportation—against the 80,000 Chechen "criminals" who lived in Russia.

Serbia

Following the collapse of communism in the former Yugoslavia and the secession of Croatia and Bosnia and Herzegovina from the Yugoslav federation in 1991–92, units of the Yugoslav army and Serbian paramilitary forces engaged in campaigns of "ethnic cleansing" aimed at driving out non-Serb majorities in northeastern Croatia and parts of northern and eastern Bosnia and establishing nominally independent Serb republics in the vacated territories. The attacks, which were compared in their ferocity and cruelty to the Nazi invasions of Eastern Europe and Russia, involved mass executions (mostly of men and boys), forced marches, torture, starvation, and systematic rape. These tactics were aimed at creating irreversible ethnic hatreds that would permanently prevent the development of multiethnic states in the areas under attack. In 1998–99 similar tactics were employed in Kosovo, a province of Serbia in which 90 percent of the population was ethnically Albanian and predominantly Muslim.

Organized and directed by the regime of Serbian president Slobodan Miloševic, leader of the Socialist Party of Serbia (Socijalisticka Partija Srbije; SPS), the campaigns in Croatia and Bosnia were undertaken in part to bolster Miloševic's image as a staunch nationalist and to consolidate his power at the expense of Vojislav Seselj's Serbian Radical Party (Srpska Radikalna Stranka; SRS), then the largest neofascist party in Serbia. Although the SPS had won 65 percent of the vote in elections to the Serbian assembly in 1990, deteriorating economic conditions and perceived threats to Serbian enclaves in Croatia and Bosnia (where Serbs constituted 12 percent and 31 percent of the population, respectively) resulted in a significant loss of support for Miloševic's SPS and a corresponding growth in the SRS and other extreme nationalist and neofascist groups. In 1992 the SPS won only 40 percent of the vote and was forced to enter into an unofficial "red-brown" alliance with the SRS, which finished with 20 percent. To counter the growing threat from the right, Miloševic gradually adopted many of the neofascists' policies, including support for the creation of a "Greater Serbia" that would incorporate Montenegro, Macedonia, and large areas of Croatia and Bosnia.

In May 1993, after a year of severe economic hardship caused by UN-imposed sanctions, Miloševic accepted

Slobodan Miloševic

Slobodan Miloševic (b. Aug. 29, 1941, Pozarevac, Yugos.– found dead March 11, 2006, The Hague, Neth.) was a politician and administrator, who, as Serbia's party leader and president (1989–97), pursued Serbian nationalist policies that contributed to the breakup of the socialist Yugoslav federation. He subsequently embroiled Serbia in a series of conflicts with the successor Balkan states. From 1997 to 2000 he served as president of the Federal Republic of Yugoslavia.

Miloševic was born in Serbia of Montenegrin parents and joined the Communist Party of Yugoslavia (from 1963 the League of Communists of Yugoslavia [LCY]) when he was 18

(continued on the next page)

Slobodan Miloševic appearing before the UN's International Criminal Tribunal for the Former Yugoslavia (ICTY) at The Hague. Raphael Gaillarde/Gamma-Rapho/Getty Images

years old. He graduated from the University of Belgrade with a law degree in 1964 and began a career in business administration, eventually becoming head of the state-owned gas company and president of a major Belgrade bank. He married Mirjana Markovic, a staunch communist who became his political adviser. Miloševic entered politics full-time in 1984 as a protégé of Ivan Stambolic, head of the League of Communists of Serbia (LCS). Miloševic took over as head of the local communist party organization in Belgrade that year.

Miloševic soon introduced a new populist political style to Serbia, appealing directly to the Serbian people over the heads of LCY officials and calling for an "antibureaucratic revolution." He used his rising popularity to oust his former mentor Stambolic as leader of the LCS in December 1987. As Serbia's party leader, Miloševic demanded that the federal government restore full control to Serbia over the autonomous provinces of Vojvodina and Kosovo. And at a time when the federal government was trying to introduce free-market reforms in order to relieve the faltering Yugoslav economy, he emerged as a leading defender of the socialist tradition of state economic intervention, attacking economic reform for its social costs.

In 1988 Miloševic replaced the party leadership in Vojvodina and Kosovo provinces with his own supporters, and in 1989 the Serbian assembly ousted Stambolic from the republic's presidency, replacing him with Miloševic. In 1990 Miloševic pushed through changes to the Serbian constitution that curtailed the provinces' autonomy. He resisted a growing movement in favour of multiparty elections, and he sought to use the extensive Serbian diaspora throughout Yugoslavia in his fight against confederalism, a looser union of sovereign republics that was advocated by the leaders of Croatia and Slovenia. But Miloševic's policies created an anti-Serb backlash in the other republics, and Serbia's continuing resistance to political and economic reform accelerated the breakup of the Yugoslav federation. The LCY split into separate republican parties in 1990, and multiparty elections later that year brought noncommunist governments to power in both Croatia and Slovenia. Miloševic transformed the LCS into the Socialist Party of Serbia and in December 1990 was returned to office by a huge majority. He was reelected to the Serbian presidency in 1992.

In 1991 Miloševic faced popularly elected leaders from Croatia and Slovenia who continued to press for the transformation of Yugoslavia into a confederation. A negotiated settlement proved impossible, and in 1991 first Slovenia and Croatia and then Macedonia declared their independence. In 1992 the Bosniaks (Muslims) and Croats of Bosnia and Herzegovina also voted to secede. In response, Miloševic backed Serbian militias who were fighting to unite Bosnia and Croatia with Serbia. After three years of full-scale warfare in Bosnia, however, Serbian militias were unable to overwhelm the Bosniak and Croatian forces there, and in 1995 the Croatian army swept almost the entire Serbian population out of its historic enclaves in Croatia. By this time Serbia's economy, which had never recovered from the political crises of the late 1980s, was suffering severely from trade sanctions that had been imposed on Yugoslavia by the United Nations (UN) in 1992. In order to lift the sanctions, Miloševic agreed on behalf of the Bosnian Serbs to a peace accord in November 1995, thus effectively ending the fighting in Bosnia.

During 1998 the long-standing dispute between Serbia and the ethnic Albanians of Kosovo deteriorated rapidly into open armed conflict between federal security forces and the guerrilla Kosovo Liberation Army, which had begun killing Serbian policemen and politicians. In the early spring of 1999 the Serbs launched a major offensive aimed at defeating the insurgents. NATO forces retaliated by initiating a massive aerial bombing campaign against Yugoslavia, expecting that Miloševic would quickly capitulate. Unexpectedly, many Serbs previously critical of his government rallied in support of their country; capitalizing on this, he ordered a program of ethnic cleansing of the Kosovar Albanians that drove hundreds of thousands of

(continued on the next page)

them into neighbouring countries as refugees. By June, however, Milošević had agreed to a peace accord with NATO that obliged him to withdraw Serbian forces from Kosovo.

As Serbia's president, Milošević had continued to dominate the new Federal Republic of Yugoslavia, which had been inaugurated in 1992 and consisted of only Serbia and Montenegro. He maintained power by his repression of political opponents, his control of the mass media, and the opportunistic alliances he formed with parties across the political spectrum, including Yugoslav United Left, the party led by his wife. Having served two terms as president of Serbia, Milošević was constitutionally barred from serving a third term. He retained power, however, by having the federal parliament elect him to the presidency of Yugoslavia in 1997. Milošević's attempt to cling to power by taking the federal presidency exposed him to indictment by the UN's International Criminal Tribunal for the Former Yugoslavia (ICTY) at The Hague. It had been difficult to charge Milošević when he was president of Serbia before 1997 with any possible offenses committed by Yugoslav troops during the war with Bosnia, but, as president of Yugoslavia, he was also the commander in chief of the federal armed forces. He was thus deemed responsible for any offenses against international law committed during the Kosovo conflict and was indicted in May 1999.

Unrest under Milošević's rule and a faltering economy grew in 2000, and in the September presidential elections he was defeated by opposition leader Vojislav Koštunica. Milošević was arrested by the Yugoslav government in 2001 and turned over to the ICTY for trial on charges of genocide, crimes against humanity, and war crimes. The trial began in February 2002 but experienced numerous delays because of the poor health of Milošević, who served as his own defense lawyer. On March 11, 2006, he was found dead in his prison cell.

an international agreement for the division of Bosnia into 10 ethnic cantons. The Vance-Owen plan (named after its principal negotiators, former U.S. secretary of state Cyrus Vance and former British foreign minister David Owen) was rejected by the self-styled parliament of the Bosnian Serbs and condemned by Seselj, who attacked Miloševic for "selling out" and called for a parliamentary vote of no confidence. Miloševic responded by launching an "antifascist" campaign against Seselj and the SRS, charging Seselj with profiteering and committing war crimes in Croatia and Bosnia and arresting several members of the SRS's paramilitary wing, the "Chetniks" (named after the Serbian nationalist guerrilla movement that battled the Nazis and later the communist Partisans in Yugoslavia during World War II). Miloševic subsequently attempted to weaken nationalist support for the SRS by allying himself with the notorious paramilitary leader Zeljko Raznatovic (popularly known by his nom de guerre, Arkan) and his new Serbian Unity Party (Srpska Partja Jedinstva; SJP). In elections in December 1993, the SPS increased its representation in the Serbian assembly at the expense of the SRS, taking 49 percent of the vote, compared with the SRS's 14 percent.

In early 1998 Serbian military and police forces began attacks in Kosovo on alleged strongholds of the Kosovo Liberation Army (KLA), an ethnically Albanian guerrilla movement fighting to end Serbian control of the province. The Serbs' harsh repression of the Albanian civilian population drew international condemnation and resulted in renewed UN sanctions on Yugoslavia. On March 24, 1999, after a Serbian delegation at peace talks in Rambouillet, France, rejected an accord that had been signed by representatives of Kosovar Albanians and the KLA, the North Atlantic Treaty Organization (NATO) began an intensive bombing campaign directed at Yugoslav military targets and later also at civilian infrastructure and government buildings in Serbia. In response, Serbian security forces in Kosovo conducted a massive campaign of ethnic cleansing, including large-scale massacres of civilians, and eventually forced more than 850,000 Kosovars to flee to border areas in Albania, Macedonia, and Montenegro. The bombing came to an end in early June after Milošević agreed to the withdrawal of Serbian forces from Kosovo, the deployment of NATO peacekeeping troops, and the repatriation of Albanian refugees. In the meantime, Milošević and four top officials of his government were indicted for crimes against humanity by the UN International Criminal Tribunal at The Hague. The trial began in February 2002 but experienced numerous delays because of the poor health of Milošević; he was found dead in his prison cell in 2006.

Croatia

In the early 1990s the main spokesman for neofascism in Croatia was Dobroslav Paraga, founder in 1990 of the Croatian Party of Rights (Hrvatska Stranka Prava; HSP). A former seminary student and dissident under the communist regime in Croatia in the 1980s, Paraga believed that Serbia was a mortal danger to Croatian national survival, and he called for the creation of a "Greater Croatia" that would include much of Serbia and all of Bosnia and Herzegovina. He insisted that war with Serbia was inevitable and had to end in the "total defeat" of the enemy with "nothing left of Serbia except Belgrade and its surroundings."

Paraga's followers openly endorsed the pro-Nazi Ustaša regime, which had carried out large-scale exterminations of Serbs, Jews, and Gypsies (Roma) in Croatia during World War II. Reflecting the enthusiasm for Ustaša symbolism that swept Croatia after the outbreak of the Bosnian war in 1991,

HSP members often wore caps marked with a U and donned black shirts in imitation of the former Ustaša paramilitary; they also gave fascist salutes and repeated the old Ustaša slogan "Ready for the homeland." The HSP's paramilitary wing, the Croatian Defense Association (Hrvatska Obrambeni Savez; HOS), was heavily involved in fighting against Serbia.

The economic program of the HSP was vague, maintaining that the principal solution to all social and economic problems was the creation of a Greater Croatia. In elections in 1992, the HSP received only about 7 percent of the parliamentary vote and Paraga only 5 percent of the presidential vote. The party's electoral impact was reduced by its insistence on continuing the unpopular war against Serbia and by Paraga's refusal to join forces with other neofascist parties in Croatia, such as the Croatian Party of Pure Rights (Hrvastska Ci sta Stranka Prava; HCSP), the Croatian Democratic Party (Hrvatgska Demokratska Stranka Prava; HDSZP), and the National Democratic League (Nacionalna Demokratska Liga; NDL).

Like the SRS in Serbia, the HSP was opposed by a larger ruling party—the Croatian Democratic Union (Hrvatska Demokratska Zajednica; HDZ), founded in 1989 by Franjo Tudjman—that eventually adopted neofascist policies in order to undercut the appeal of its extreme nationalist and neofascist rivals. Like the HSP, the Tudjman regime employed many Ustaša symbols, and it even rehabilitated many Ustaša leaders and nominated some of them to government posts. The HDZ incorporated into its ranks the Croatian National Committee, a group founded by Ranimir Jelic, a close associate of Ante Pavelic, the founder of the original Ustaša. In 1995 Tudjman's troops undertook extensive ethnic cleansing campaigns in western Slavonia and the historically Serbian region of Krajina, forcing the evacuation of some 150,000 Croatian Serbs to Serbia and Serb-held areas of Bosnia.

Beginning in 1991, Tudjman took various repressive measures against the HSP, including the arrest of Paraga on charges of having formed an illegal paramilitary group and the formal incorporation of the HOS into the regular Croatian army. In 1993 the government launched a largely successful "antifascist" campaign aimed at curbing the influence of HSP supporters in the military. In the same year, Paraga was brought to trial for having allegedly plotted a coup, though he was later acquitted.

Neofascism Outside Europe

The largest neofascist movements outside Europe after World War II emerged in Latin America, South Africa, and the Middle East. Juan Perón, who ruled Argentina as the legally elected president in 1946–55 and again in 1973–74, served as a military attaché to Italy in the 1930s and was a great admirer of the duce. As he later said, "Mussolini was the greatest man of our century, but he committed certain disastrous errors. I, who have the advantage of his precedent before me, shall follow in his footsteps but also avoid his errors."

Perón won the support of poor industrial workers (the *descamisados*, or "shirtless ones") as well as many wealthy businessmen by promoting higher wages and benefits as well as industrial development. He also had the backing of many middle-class nationalists and a large portion of the army officer corps. His charismatic wife, Eva Perón, popularly known as Evita, attracted a cult following for her charitable activities and her storybook rise from "rags to riches." However, owing to inflation, corruption, and Perón's conflicts with the formerly dominant landowning class and the Catholic Church, the military eventually turned against him, and he was ousted in a coup in 1955.

After a long exile in Spain, Perón returned to Argentina in 1973 and, in a special election in October of that year, was elected president with his second wife, Isabel Perón, as vice president. Succeeding her husband after his death in 1974, Isabel Perón could not prevent a split between rightist and leftist factions of the Peronist coalition. The economy deteriorated dramatically, with inflation reaching triple digits by 1975, and the country was plagued by waves of kidnappings and assassinations of government and business leaders by leftist guerrillas—violence that was soon answered in kind, and on a much larger scale, by the military and secret police. Having lost all popular support, Isabel Perón was overthrown in a military coup in March 1976.

The most significant neofascist group in South Africa after 1945 was the South African Gentile National Socialist Movement (the "Greyshirts"), which changed its name to the White Workers Party in 1949. Although the party did not succeed in creating a mass movement, it did encourage the adoption of policies of white supremacy and apartheid by the dominant National Party of South Africa.

In the Middle East the regimes of Muammar al-Qaddafi in Libya and Ṣaddām Ḥussein in Iraq were neofascist in several respects. A charismatic dictator and devout Muslim, Qaddafi came to power in 1969 in a military coup that overthrew King Idris. He advocated what he called "true democracy," characterized by state ownership of key sectors of the economy, strict adherence to Islamic law, and the mobilization of mass support through "people's congresses," government-controlled labour unions, and other organizations. In Iraq, Ḥussein's Baʿth movement defended an extremely nationalistic brand of socialism that rejected Western liberalism as well as "materialistic communism." Ḥussein's regime, which came to power in a coup in 1968, was essentially a personal dictatorship based on an Arab version of the *Führerprinzip*.

Ba'th Party

The Ba'th party is an Arab political party advocating the formation of a single Arab socialist nation. It has branches in many Middle Eastern countries and was the ruling party in Syria from 1963 and in Iraq from 1968 to 2003.

The Ba'th Party was founded in 1943 in Damascus, Syria, by Michel 'Aflaq and Salah al-Din al-Bitār, adopted its constitution in 1947, and in 1953 merged with the Syrian Socialist Party to form the Arab Socialist Ba'th (Renaissance) Party. The Ba'th Party espoused nonalignment and opposition to imperialism and colonialism, took inspiration from what

Thirty-foot-tall bronze sculptures of former Iraqi dictator Ṣaddām Ḥussein, on the grounds of the Republican Palace, Baghdad, 2005. Jim Gordon, CIV/U.S. Department of Defense

it considered the positive values of Islam, and attempted to ignore or transcend class divisions. Its structure was highly centralized and authoritarian.

The Syrian Baʿthists took power in 1963, but factionalism between "progressives" and "nationalists" was severe until 1970, when Ḥafiz al-Assad of the "nationalists" secured control. In Iraq the Baʿthists took power briefly in 1963 and regained it in 1968, after which the party's power became concentrated under Iraqi leader Ṣaddām Ḥussein. Differences between the Iraqi and Syrian wings of the Baʿth Party precluded unification of the two countries. Within both countries the Baʿthists formed fronts with smaller parties, including at times the communists. In Syria the main internal threat to Baʿth hegemony stemmed from the Muslim Brotherhood, while in Iraq Kurdish and Shīʿite opposition was endemic. The Iraqi branch of the party was toppled in 2003 as a result of the Iraq War.

In the 1990s a number of racist "militia" groups were active in the United States, and many of them made use of paramilitary uniforms and neo-Nazi symbolism. However, they lacked the popular support necessary to launch a strong political movement or to engage in electoral politics on their own.

CHAPTER 5

TOTALITARIANISM

Totalitarianism is a form of government that theoretically permits no individual freedom and that seeks to subordinate all aspects of the individual's life to the authority of the government. Italian dictator Benito Mussolini coined the term *totalitario* in the early 1920s to describe the new fascist state of Italy, which he further described as: "All within the state, none outside the state, none against the state." By the beginning of World War II, "totalitarian" had become synonymous with absolute and oppressive single-party government.

In the broadest sense, totalitarianism is characterized by strong central rule that attempts to control and direct all aspects of individual life through coercion and repression. Examples of such centralized totalitarian rule include the Maurya dynasty of India (*c.* 321–c. 185 BCE), the Ch'in dynasty of China (221–206 BCE), and the reign of Zulu chief Shaka (*c.* 1816–28). The totalitarian states of Nazi Germany under Adolf Hitler (1933–45) and the Soviet Union under Joseph Stalin (1924–53) were the first examples of decentralized or popular totalitarianism, in which the state achieved overwhelming popular support for its leadership. This support was not spontaneous; its genesis depended on a charismatic leader; and it was made possible only by modern developments in communication and transportation.

Other experiments in totalitarianism include Albania under Enver Hoxha and North Korea under Kim Il Sung

Mauryan Empire

The Mauryan empire (*c.* 321–185 BCE), was, in ancient India, a state centred at Pataliputra (later Patna) near the junction of the Son and Ganges (Ganga) rivers. In the wake of Alexander the Great's death, Chandragupta (or Chandragupta Maurya), its dynastic founder, carved out the majority of an empire that encompassed most of the subcontinent except for the Tamil south. The Mauryan empire was an efficient and highly organized autocracy with a standing army and civil service. This bureaucracy and its operation were the model for the *Artha-shastra* ("The Science of Material Gain"), a work of political

(continued on the next page)

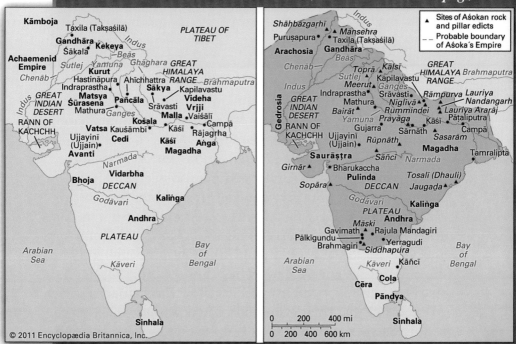

In about 500 BCE (left) *India was ruled by many local chiefs and kings. After about 321 BCE the Mauryan family created a unified empire. The Mauryan empire reached its largest size in about 250 BCE* (right; area colored brown), *under the emperor Ashoka.* Encyclopædia Britannica, Inc.

economy similar in tone and scope to Niccolò Machiavelli's *The Prince*.

Much is known of the reign of the Buddhist Mauryan emperor Ashoka (reigned *c.* 265–238 BCE or *c.* 273–232 BCE) from the exquisitely executed stone edicts that he had erected throughout his realm. These comprise some of the oldest deciphered original texts of India. Ashoka campaigned little to expand the realm; rather, his conquest consisted of sending many Buddhist emissaries throughout Asia and commissioning some of the finest works of ancient Indian art.

After Ashoka's death the empire shrank because of invasions, defections by southern princes, and quarrels over ascension. The last ruler, Brihadratha, was killed in 185 BCE by his Brahman commander in chief, Pushyamitra, who then founded the Shunga dynasty, which ruled in central India for about a century.

after the end of World War II, and Vietnam and Cambodia after the end of the Vietnam War in 1975. Of these states, Albania had the distinction of being an almost completely closed society until 1990. It had relations with very few other nations, not even with similar communist states.

In a number of other countries the attempt to assert totalitarian control had mixed success. Among these were Yugoslavia, Romania, Bulgaria, Hungary, Poland, East Germany, and Czechoslovakia. Of these, Romania probably had the most repressive government, while those of other former Soviet-bloc nations found it useful to allow their citizens some freedoms so that their economies could prosper.

The experience in China is unique in modern times. It underwent a communist revolution in 1949, and Mao Zedong tried to transform the country into a totalitarian state after the pattern of Joseph Stalin in the Soviet Union. He had a great measure of success, keeping the country in a state of revolutionary turmoil and economic stagnation until the early 1970s. After his death in 1976 his political and economic goals were abandoned as unworkable.

Totalitarianism differs from authoritarianism, since authoritarian governments usually have no highly developed guiding ideology, tolerate some pluralism in social organization, lack the power to mobilize the entire population in pursuit of national goals, and exercise that power within relatively predictable limits. Examples of authoritarian regimes, according to some scholars, include the pro-Western military dictatorships that existed in Latin America and elsewhere in the second half of the 20th century.

Totalitarianism is also often distinguished from dictatorship, despotism, or tyranny by its supplanting of all political institutions with new ones and its sweeping away of all legal, social, and political traditions. The totalitarian state pursues some special goal, such as industrialization or conquest, to the exclusion of all others. All resources are directed toward its attainment regardless of the cost. Whatever might further the goal is supported; whatever might foil the goal is rejected. This obsession spawns an ideology that explains everything in terms of the goal, rationalizing all obstacles that may arise and all forces that may contend with the state. The resulting popular support permits the state the widest latitude of action of any form of government. Any dissent is branded evil, and internal political differences are not permitted. Because pursuit of the goal is the only ideological foundation for the totalitarian state, achievement of the goal can never be acknowledged.

Maintaining Control

Modern totalitarian countries have been made possible, at least in part, by the revolution in communications and transportation in the 20th century. Radio, motion pictures, and television have proved invaluable as ways to spread propaganda, or government-sponsored truth, to tell citizens what the government wants them to hear about their own country and their country's enemies. Electronic devices are useful for surveillance to keep watch on the public and to monitor all telephone calls.

Government ownership and operation of transportation systems make it possible to control the movements of the population and to move military forces rapidly to any place they may be needed. Germany's modern autobahns, or highways, for example, were designed by Hitler's engineers in the 1930s precisely for the purpose of speeding the movement of military transport.

Under totalitarian rule, traditional social institutions and organizations are discouraged and suppressed; thus the social fabric is weakened and people become more amenable to absorption into a single, unified movement. Participation in approved public organizations is at first encouraged and then required. Old religious and social ties are supplanted by artificial ties to the state and its ideology. As pluralism and individualism diminish, most of the people embrace the totalitarian state's ideology. The infinite diversity among individuals blurs, replaced by a mass conformity (or at least acquiescence) to the beliefs and behaviour sanctioned by the state.

Large-scale, organized violence becomes permissible and sometimes necessary under totalitarian rule, justified by the overriding commitment to the state ideology and pursuit of the state's goal. In Nazi Germany and Stalin's Soviet Union, whole classes of people, such as the Jews and the kulaks (wealthy peasant farmers) respectively, were singled out for persecution and extinction. In each case the persecuted were linked with some external enemy and blamed for the state's troubles, and thereby public opinion was aroused against them and their fate at the hands of the military and the police was condoned.

Police operations within a totalitarian state often appear similar to those within a police state, but one important difference distinguishes them. In a police state the police operate according to known, consistent procedures. In a totalitarian state the police operate without the constraints of laws and regulations. Their actions are unpredictable and directed by the whim of their rulers. Under Hitler and Stalin uncertainty was interwoven into the affairs of the state. The German constitution of the Weimar Republic was never abrogated under Hitler, but an enabling act passed by the Reichstag in 1933 permitted him to amend the constitution at will, in effect nullifying it. The role of lawmaker became vested in one man. Similarly, Stalin provided a constitution for the Soviet Union in 1936 but never permitted it to become the framework of Soviet law. Instead, he was the final arbiter in the interpretation of Marxism–Leninism–Stalinism and changed his interpretations at will. Neither Hitler nor Stalin permitted change to become predictable, thus increasing the sense of terror among the people and repressing any dissent.

Goals of the Government

The most widely known totalitarian ideology in the 20th century was Marxism, or communism. Unfortunately, Karl Marx and his followers never spelled out, except in the vaguest way, what kind of society would result if their beliefs were put into practice. Their concern was criticizing capitalism and seeking ways to overturn it. With what they would replace it was never clarified.

However imprecisely the goals are stated, all of the energies of the state are devoted to building communism, whatever the cost to those who are given the work of doing it. Marx, Vladimir Lenin, and others have stated that communism is the goal toward which all human history is inevitably moving. Any obstacles in reaching this goal must be removed by the government, and every citizen must be shown a place in the working out of this historical process.

Marxism

The fundamental ideology of communism, Marxism holds that all people are entitled to enjoy the fruits of their labour but are prevented from doing so in a capitalist economic system, which divides society into two classes: nonowning workers and nonworking owners. Marx called the resulting situation "alienation," and he said that when the workers repossessed the fruits of their labour, alienation would be overcome and class divisions would cease. The Marxist theory of history posits class struggle as history's driving force, and it sees capitalism as the most recent and most critical historical stage—most critical because at this stage the proletariat will at last arise united. The failure of the European Revolutions of 1848 and an increasing need to elaborate on Marxist theory, whose orientation is more analytical than practical, led to adaptations such as Leninism and Maoism. In the late 20th century the collapse of the Soviet Union and its Eastern bloc allies seemed to mark the end of Soviet Marxism as a practical political or economic model. Meanwhile, China adopted many elements of a free-market economy in what it called a development rather than a repudiation of Marxist theory. In the West, Marxism continues to be appreciated as a critique of market capitalism and a theory of historical change.

Totalitarianism in Practice

If communist ideology is vague, Hitler's goals were very clear. They were primarily two. First was the necessary and inevitable movement of the German people to the east to conquer lands they would need in the future as their population expanded. This resulted in the waging of war against the Soviet Union. Second was the "purification" of the population.

In the Soviet Union, Leninism resulted in the creation of a totalitarian state. After Lenin's death, in January 1924, Stalin promoted an extravagant, quasi-Byzantine cult of the deceased leader. Archpriest of Leninism, Stalin also promoted his own cult in the following year. Chief architect of Soviet totalitarianism and a skilled but phenomenally ruthless organizer, he destroyed the remnants of individual freedom and failed to promote individual prosperity, yet he created a mighty military–industrial complex and led the Soviet Union into the nuclear age.

In the second half of the 20th century, another powerful form of totalitarian ideology reasserted itself in several parts of the world—religious fundamentalism. In the Middle East, Islamic fundamentalists had great success in Iran by overthrowing the government of the shah in 1979 and proclaiming an Islamic republic. The new government, led by the Ayatollah Ruhollah Khomeini, became one of the most brutal and oppressive in the modern world. Its success in maintaining power led Islamic fundamentalists in other nearby nations to aim at a similar goal. In every country where there is a large population of Muslims, there has been a resurgence of religious fundamentalism, and governments have been forced to make concessions to it in order to stay in power.

National Socialism

National Socialism (German: *Nationalsozialismus*, also called Nazism or Naziism) was a totalitarian movement led by Adolf Hitler as head of the Nazi Party in Germany. In its intense nationalism, mass appeal, and dictatorial rule, National Socialism shared many elements with Italian fascism. However, Nazism was far more extreme both in its ideas and in its practice. In almost every respect it was an anti-intellectual and atheoretical movement, emphasizing the will of the charismatic dictator as the sole source of inspiration of a people and a nation, as well as a vision of annihilation of all enemies of the Aryan *Volk* as the one and only goal of Nazi policy.

The Roots of National Socialism

National Socialism had peculiarly German roots. It can be partly traced to the Prussian tradition as developed under Frederick William I (1688–1740), Frederick the Great (1712–68), and Otto von Bismarck (1815–98), which regarded the militant spirit and the discipline of the Prussian army as the model for all individual and civic life. To it was added the tradition of political romanticism, with its sharp hostility to rationalism and to the principles underlying the French Revolution, its emphasis on instinct and the past, and its proclamation of the rights of Friedrich Nietzsche's exceptional individual (the *Übermensch* ["Superman"]) over all universal law and rules. These two traditions were later reinforced by the 19th-century adoration of science and of the laws of nature, which seemed to operate independently of all concepts of good and evil. Further reinforcements came from such 19th-century intellectual figures as the comte de Gobineau (1816–82), Richard Wagner (1813–83), and Houston Stewart Chamberlain (1855–1927), all of whom greatly influenced early National Socialism with their claims of the racial and cultural superiority of the "Nordic" (Germanic) peoples over all other Europeans and all other races.

Hitler's intellectual viewpoint was influenced during his youth not only by these currents in the German tradition but also by specific Austrian movements that professed various political sentiments, notably those of pan-Germanic expansionism and anti-Semitism. Hitler's ferocious nationalism, his contempt of the Slavs, and his hatred of the Jews can largely be explained by his bitter experiences as an unsuccessful artist living a threadbare existence on the streets of Vienna, the capital of the multiethnic Austro-Hungarian Empire.

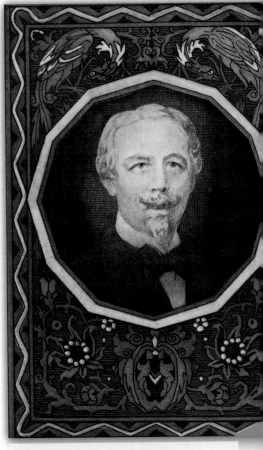

Joseph-Arthur, comte de Gobineau. Nouvelles Asiatiques, by Joseph-Arthur de Gobineau; edition G. Crés, 1924

This intellectual preparation would probably not have been sufficient for the growth of National Socialism in Germany but for that country's defeat in World War I. The defeat and the resulting disillusionment, pauperization, and frustration—particularly among the lower middle classes—paved the way for the success of the propaganda of Hitler and the Nazis. The Treaty of Versailles (1919), the formal settlement of World War I drafted without German participation, alienated many Germans with its imposition of harsh monetary and territorial reparations. The significant resentment expressed toward the peace treaty gave Hitler a starting point. Because German representatives (branded the "November criminals" by National Socialists) agreed to cease hostilities and did not unconditionally surrender in the armistice of November 11, 1918, there was a widespread feeling—particularly in the military—that Germany's defeat had been orchestrated by diplomats at the Versailles meetings. From the beginning, Hitler's propaganda of revenge for this "traitorous" act, through which the German people had been "stabbed in the back," and his call for rearmament had strong appeal within military circles, which regarded the peace only as a temporary setback in Germany's expansionist program. The ruinous inflation of the German currency in 1923 wiped out the savings of many middle-class households and led to further public alienation and dissatisfaction.

Hitler added to Pan-Germanic aspirations the almost mystical fanaticism of a faith in the mission of the German race and the fervour of a social revolutionary gospel. This gospel was most fully expressed in Hitler's personal testament *Mein Kampf* (1925–27; "My Struggle"), in which he outlined both his practical aims and his theories of race and propaganda.

Posing as a bulwark against communism, Hitler exploited the fears aroused in Germany and worldwide by the Bolshevik Revolution in Russia and the consolidation of communist power in the Soviet Union. Thus, he was able to secure the support of many conservative elements that misunderstood the totalitarian character of his movement.

Hitler's most important individual contribution to the theory and practice of National Socialism was his deep understanding of mass psychology and mass propaganda. He stressed the fact that all propaganda must hold its intellectual level at the capacity of the least intelligent of those at whom it is directed and that its truthfulness is much less important than its success. According to Hitler:

It is part of a great leader's genius to make even widely separated adversaries appear as if they belonged to but one category because among weakly and undecided characters the recognition of various enemies all too easily marks the beginning of doubt of one's own rightness.

Hitler found this common denominator in the Jews, whom he identified with both Bolshevism and a kind of cosmic evil. The Jews were to be discriminated against not according to their religion but according to their "race." National Socialism declared the Jews—whatever their educational and social development—to be forever fundamentally different from and inimical to Germans.

National Socialism attempted to reconcile conservative, nationalist ideology with a socially radical doctrine. In so doing, it became a profoundly revolutionary movement—albeit a largely negative one. Rejecting rationalism, liberalism, democracy, the rule of law, human rights, and all movements of international cooperation and peace, it stressed instinct, the subordination of the individual to the state, and the necessity of blind and unswerving obedience to leaders appointed from above. It also emphasized the inequality of men and races and the right of the strong to rule the weak; sought to purge or suppress competing political, religious, and social institutions; advanced an ethic of hardness and ferocity; and partly destroyed class distinctions by drawing into the movement misfits and failures from all social classes. Although socialism was traditionally an internationalist creed, the radical wing of National Socialism knew that a mass base existed for policies that were simultaneously anticapitalist and nationalist. However, after Hitler secured power, this radical strain was eliminated.

Totalitarianism and Expansionism

Working from these principles, Hitler carried his party from its inauspicious beginnings in a beer cellar in Munich to a dominant position in world politics 20 years later. The Nazi Party originated in 1919 and was led by Hitler from 1920. Through both successful electioneering and intimidation, the party came to power in Germany in 1933 and governed through totalitarian methods until 1945, when Hitler committed suicide and Germany was defeated and occupied by the Allies at the close of World War II.

Adolf Hitler speaking at a rally. Hulton Archive/Getty Images

The history of National Socialism after 1934 can be divided into two periods of about equal length. Between 1934 and 1939 the party established full control of all phases of life in Germany. With many Germans weary of party conflicts, economic and political instability, and the disorderly freedom that characterized the last years of the Weimar Republic (1919–33), Hitler and his movement gained the support and even the enthusiasm of a majority of the German population. In particular, the public welcomed the strong, decisive, and apparently effective government provided by the Nazis. Germany's endless ranks of unemployed rapidly dwindled as the jobless were put to work in extensive public-works projects and in rapidly multiplying armaments factories. Germans were swept up in this orderly, intensely purposeful mass movement bent on restoring their country to its dignity, pride, and grandeur, as well as to dominance on the European stage. Economic recovery from the effects of the Great Depression and the forceful assertion of German nationalism were key factors in National Socialism's appeal to the German population. Further, Hitler's continuous string of diplomatic successes and foreign conquests from 1934 through the early years of World War II secured the unqualified support of most Germans, including many who had previously opposed him.

Despite its economic and political success, National Socialism maintained its power by coercion and mass manipulation. The Nazi regime disseminated a continual outpouring of propaganda through all cultural and informational media. Its rallies—especially its elaborately staged Nürnberg rallies—its insignia, and its uniformed cadres were designed to impart an aura of omnipotence. The underside of its propaganda machine was its apparatus of terror, with its ubiquitous secret police and concentration camps. It fanned and focused German anti-Semitism to make the Jews a symbol of all that was hated and feared. By means of deceptive rhetoric, the party portrayed the Jews as the enemy of all classes of society.

National Socialism's principal instrument of control was the unification, under Heinrich Himmler and his chief lieutenant, Reinhard Heydrich, of the SS (the uniformed police force of the Nazi Party) and all other police and security organizations. Opposition to the regime was destroyed either by outright terror or, more frequently, by the all-pervading fear of possible repression. Opponents of the regime were branded enemies of the state and of the people, and an elaborate web of informers— often members of the family or intimate friends—imposed utmost caution on all expressions and activities. Justice was no longer recognized as objective but was completely subordinated to the alleged needs and interests of the *Volk*. In addition to the now-debased methods of the normal judicial process, special detention camps were erected. In these camps the SS exercised supreme authority and introduced a system of sadistic brutality unrivaled in modern times.

Between 1938 and 1945 Hitler's regime attempted to expand and apply the Nazi system to territories outside the German Reich. This endeavour was confined, in 1938, to

SS Guard

The *Schutzstaffel* (German: "Protective Echelon"), abbreviated SS, was the black-uniformed elite corps of the Nazi Party. Founded by Adolf Hitler in April 1925 as a small personal bodyguard, the SS grew with the success of the Nazi movement and, gathering immense police and military powers, became virtually a state within a state.

From 1929 until its dissolution in 1945, the SS was headed by Heinrich Himmler, who built up the SS from fewer than 300 members to more than 50,000 by the time the Nazis came to

An SS honour guard. FPG/Archive Photos/Getty Images

power in 1933. Himmler, a racist fanatic, screened applicants for their supposed physical perfection and racial purity but recruited members from all ranks of German society. With their sleek black uniforms and special insignia (lightning-like runic S's, death's head badges, and silver daggers), the men of the SS felt superior to the brawling brown-shirted Storm Troopers of the SA, to which initially they were nominally subordinate.

When Hitler, with SS help, purged the SA in 1934 and reduced it to political impotence, the SS became an independent group responsible, via Himmler, to Hitler alone. Between

(continued on the next page)

1934 and 1936 Himmler and his chief adjutant, Reinhard Heydrich, consolidated SS strength by gaining control of all of Germany's police forces and expanding their organization's responsibilities and activities. At the same time, special military SS units were trained and equipped along the lines of the regular army. By 1939 the SS, now numbering about 250,000 men, had become a massive and labyrinthian bureaucracy, divided mainly into two groups: the Allgemeine-SS (General SS) and the Waffen-SS (Armed SS).

The Allgemeine-SS dealt mainly with police and "racial" matters. Its most important division was the Reichssicherheitshauptamt (RSHA; Reich Security Central Office), which was made up of the Ordnungspolizei (Orpo; Order Police) and the Sicherheitspolizei (Sipo; Security Police), which, in turn, was divided into the Kriminalpolizei (Kripo; Criminal Police) and the dreaded Gestapo under Heinrich Müller. The RSHA also included the Sicherheitsdienst (SD; Security Service), a security department in charge of foreign and domestic intelligence and espionage.

The Waffen-SS was made up of three subgroups: the Leibstandarte, Hitler's personal bodyguard; the Totenkopfverbände (Death's-Head Battalions), which administered the concentration camps; and the Verfügungstruppen (Disposition Troops), which swelled to 39 divisions in World War II and which, serving as elite combat troops alongside the regular army, gained a reputation as fanatical fighters.

SS men were schooled in racial hatred and admonished to harden their hearts to human suffering. Their chief "virtue" was their absolute obedience and loyalty to the Führer, who gave them their motto: "Thy Honour is Thy Loyalty." During World War II the SS carried out massive executions of political opponents, Gypsies, Jews, Polish leaders, Communist authorities, partisan resisters, and Russian prisoners of war. Following the defeat of Nazi Germany by the Allies, the SS was declared a criminal organization by the Allied Tribunal in Nürnberg in 1946.

lands inhabited by German-speaking populations, but in 1939 Germany began to subjugate non-German-speaking nationalities as well. Germany's invasion of Poland on September 1, which initiated World War II, was the logical outcome of Hitler's plans. His first years were spent in preparing the Germans for the approaching struggle for world control and in forging the military and industrial superiority that Germany would require to fulfill its ambitions. With mounting diplomatic and military successes, his aims grew in quick progression. The first was to unite all people of German descent within their historical homeland on the basis of "self-determination." His next step foresaw the creation, through the military conquest of Poland and other Slavic nations to the east, of a *Grosswirtschaftsraum* ("large economic unified space") or a *Lebensraum* ("living space"), which thereby would allow Germany to acquire sufficient territory to become economically self-sufficient and militarily impregnable. There the German master race, or *Herrenvolk*, would rule over a hierarchy of subordinate peoples and organize and exploit them with ruthlessness and efficiency. With the initial successes of the military campaigns of 1939–41, his plan was expanded into a vision of a hemispheric order that would embrace all of Europe, western Asia, and Africa and eventually the entire world.

The extravagant hopes of Nazism came to an end with Germany's defeat in 1945, after nearly six years of war. To a certain extent World War II had repeated the pattern of World War I: great initial German military successes, the forging of a large-scale coalition against Germany as the result of German ambitions and behaviour, and the eventual loss of the war because of German overreaching. National Socialism as a mass movement effectively ended on April 30, 1945, when Hitler committed suicide to avoid falling into the hands of Soviet troops completing the occupation of Berlin. Out of the ruins of National Socialism arose a Germany that was divided until 1990. Remnants of National Social-ist ideology remained in Germany after Hitler's suicide, and a small number of Nazi-oriented political parties and other groups were formed in West Germany from the late 1940s, though some were later banned. In the 1990s gangs of neo-Nazi youths in eastern Germany staged attacks against immigrants, desecrated Jewish cemeteries, and engaged in violent confrontations with leftists and police.

Leninism

Leninism refers to the principles expounded by Vladimir I. Lenin—the preeminent figure in the Russian Revolution of 1917—to guide the transition of society from capitalism to communism. Whether Leninist concepts represented a con-tribution to or a corruption of Marxist thought has been debated, but their influence on the subsequent development of communism in the Soviet Union and elsewhere has been of fundamental importance.

In the *Communist Manifesto* (1848), Karl Marx and Fried-rich Engels defined communists as "the most advanced and resolute section of the working-class parties of every coun-try, that section which pushes forward all others." This con-ception was fundamental to Leninist thought. Lenin saw the Communist Party as a highly committed intellectual elite who (1) had a scientific understanding of history and society in the light of Marxist principles, (2) were committed to end-ing capitalism and instituting socialism in its place, (3) were bent on forcing through this transition after having achieved political power, and (4) were committed to attaining this power by any means possible, including violence and revolu-tion if necessary. Lenin's emphasis upon action by a small, deeply committed group stemmed both from the need for efficiency and discretion in the revolutionary movement and from an authoritarian bent that was present in all of his political thought. The authoritarian aspect of Leninism appeared also in its insistence upon the need for a "proletarian dictatorship" following the seizure of power, a dictatorship that in practice was exercised not by the workers but by the leaders of the Communist Party.

At the root of Leninist authoritarianism was a distrust of spontaneity, a conviction that historical events, if left to themselves, would not bring the desired outcome—*i.e.*, the coming into being of a socialist society. Lenin was not at all convinced, for instance, that the workers would inevitably acquire the proper revolutionary and class consciousness of the communist elite; he was instead afraid that they would be content with the gains in living and working conditions obtained through trade-union activity. In this, Leninism differed from traditional Marxism, which predicted that material conditions would suffice to make workers conscious of the need for revolution. For Lenin, then, the communist elite— the "workers' vanguard"—was more than a catalytic agent that precipitated events along their inevitable course; it was an indispensable element.

Just as Leninism was pragmatic in its choice of means to achieve political power, it was also opportunistic in the policies it adopted and the compromises it made to maintain its hold on power. A good example of this is Lenin's own New Economic Policy (1921–28), which temporarily restored the market economy and some private enterprise in the Soviet Union after the disastrous economic results of War Communism (1918–21).

In practice, Leninism's unrestrained pursuit of the socialist society resulted in the creation of a totalitarian state in the Soviet Union. If the conditions of Russia in its backward state of development did not lead to socialism naturally, then, after coming to power, the Bolsheviks would legislate socialism into existence and would exercise despotic control to break public resistance. Thus, every aspect of the Soviet Union's political, economic, cultural, and intellectual life came to be regulated by the Communist Party in a strict and regimented fashion that would tolerate no opposition. The building of the socialist society proceeded under a new autocracy of Communist Party officials and bureaucrats. Marxism and Leninism originally expected that, with the triumph of the proletariat, the state that Marx had defined as the organ of class rule would "wither away" because class conflicts would come to an end. Communist rule in the Soviet Union resulted instead in the vastly increased power of the state apparatus. Terror was applied without hesitation, humanitarian considerations and individual rights were disregarded, and the assumption of the class character of all intellectual and moral life led to a relativization of the standards of truth, ethics, and justice. Leninism thus created the first modern totalitarian state.

Stalinism

Stalinism—the method of rule, or policies, of Joseph Stalin—is associated with a regime of terror and totalitarian rule. In a party dominated by intellectuals and rhetoricians, Stalin stood for a practical approach to revolution, devoid of ideological sentiment. Once power was in Bolshevik hands, the party leadership gladly left to Stalin tasks involving the dry details of party and state administration. In the power struggle that followed Vladimir Lenin's death in 1924, the intellectual sophistication and charismatic appeal of Stalin's rivals proved no match for the actual power he had consolidated from positions of direct control of the party machinery. By 1929 his major opponents were defeated; and Stalinist policies, which had undergone several shifts during the power struggle, became stabilized. Stalin's doctrine of the monolithic party emerged during the battle for power; he condemned the "rotten liberalism" of those who tolerated discussion on or dissent from party policies. Lenin's pronouncements, except those uncomplimentary to Stalin, were codified as axioms not open to question. Persons opposed to these new dogmas were accused of treason to the party. What came to be called the "cult of personality" developed as Stalin, presenting himself as Lenin's heir, came to be recognized as the sole infallible interpreter of party ideology.

Basic to Stalinism was the doctrine of "socialism in one country," which held that, though the socialist goal of world proletarian revolution was not to be abandoned, a viable classless society could be built within Soviet boundaries and

Joseph Stalin

Joseph Stalin (b. Dec. 18, 1879, Gori, Georgia, Russian Empire–d. March 5, 1953, Moscow, Russia, U.S.S.R.) was of Georgian—not Russian—origin, and persistent rumours claim that he was Ossetian on the paternal side. His original name was Ioseb Dzhugashvili. He was the son of a poor cobbler in the provincial Georgian town of Gori in the Caucasus, then an imperial Russian colony. He studied at a seminary but was expelled for revolutionary activity in 1899.

Stalin joined an underground revolutionary group and sided with the Bolshevik faction of the Russian Social-Democratic Workers' Party in 1903. A disciple of Vladimir Lenin, he served in minor party posts and was appointed to the first Bolshevik Central Committee (1912). He remained active behind the scenes and in exile (1913–17) until the Russian Revolution of 1917 brought the Bolsheviks to power. Having adopted the name Stalin (from Russian *stal*, "steel"), he served as commissar for nationalities and for state control in the Bolshevik government

(continued on the next page)

Joseph Stalin. Photos.com/Thinkstock

(1917–23). He was a member of the Politburo, and in 1922 he became secretary-general of the party's Central Committee.

After Lenin's death (1924), Stalin overcame his rivals, including Leon Trotsky, Grigory Zinovyev, Lev Kamenev, Nikolay Bukharin, and Aleksey Rykov, and took control of Soviet politics. In 1928 he inaugurated the Five-Year Plans that radically altered Soviet economic and social structures and resulted in the deaths of many millions. In the 1930s he contrived to eliminate threats to his power through the purge trials and through widespread secret executions and persecution. In World War II he signed the German-Soviet Nonaggression Pact (1939), attacked Finland, and annexed parts of Eastern Europe to strengthen his western frontiers.

When Germany invaded Russia (1941), Stalin took control of military operations. He allied Russia with Britain and the United States; at the Tehran, Yalta, and Potsdam conferences, he demonstrated his negotiating skill. After the war he consolidated Soviet power in Eastern Europe and built up the Soviet Union as a world military power.

Stalin continued his repressive political measures to control internal dissent; increasingly paranoid, he was preparing to mount another purge after the so-called Doctors' Plot when he died. Noted for bringing the Soviet Union into world prominence, at terrible cost to his own people, he left a legacy of repression and fear as well as industrial and military power. In 1956 Stalin and his personality cult were denounced by Nikita Khrushchev.

despite encirclement by a largely capitalist world. Stalin, appealing both to socialist revolutionary fervour and to Russian nationalism, launched in the late 1920s a program of rapid industrial development of unprecedented magnitude. A "class war" was declared on the rich farmers in the name of the poor, and Russian agriculture was rapidly collectivized, against considerable rural resistance, to meet the needs of urban industry. The need for expertise and efficiency in industry postponed the egalitarian goals of the Bolshevik Revolution; Stalin denounced "levelers" and instituted systems of reward that established a socioeconomic stratification favouring the technical intelligentsia. Heavy industry was emphasized to ensure Russia's future economic independence from its capitalist neighbours.

In 1928 Stalin abandoned Lenin's quasi-capitalist New Economic Policy in favour of headlong state-organized industrialization under a succession of Five-Year Plans. This was, in effect, a new Russian revolution more devastating in its effects than those of 1917. The dictator's blows fell most heavily on the peasantry, some 25,000,000 rustic households being compelled to amalgamate in collective or state farms within a few years. Resisting desperately, the reluctant muzhiks (peasants) were attacked by troops and OGPU (political police) units. Uncooperative peasants, termed *kulaks*, were arrested en masse, being shot, exiled, or absorbed into the rapidly expanding network of Stalinist concentration camps and worked to death under atrocious conditions. Collectivization also caused a great famine in the Ukraine. Yet Stalin continued to export the grain stocks that a less cruel leader would have rushed to the famine-stricken areas. Some 10,000,000 peasants may have perished through his policies during these years.

Crash industrialization was less disastrous in its effects, but it, too, numbered its grandiose failures, to which Stalin responded by arraigning industrial managers in a succession of show trials. Intimidated into confessing imaginary

Gulag

Gulag (abbreviation of *Glavnoye Upravleniye Ispravitelno-trudovykh Lagerey* [Russian: "Chief Administration of Corrective Labour Camps"]), refers to the system of Soviet labour camps and accompanying detention and transit camps and prisons that from the 1920s to the mid-1950s housed the political prisoners and criminals of the Soviet Union. At its height the Gulag imprisoned millions of people. The name *Gulag* had been largely unknown in the West until the publication of Aleksandr Solzhenitsyn's *The Gulag Archipelago, 1918–1956* (1973), whose title likens the labour camps scattered through the Soviet Union to an island chain.

A system of forced-labour camps was first inaugurated by a Soviet decree of April 15, 1919, and underwent a series of administrative and organizational changes in the 1920s, ending with the founding of Gulag in 1930 under the control of the secret police, OGPU (later, the NKVD and the KGB). The Gulag had a total inmate population of about 100,000 in the late 1920s, when it underwent an enormous expansion coinciding with the Soviet

The barracks of a forced labour camp—part of the Gulag—in Siberia. Sovfoto/ Universal Images Group/Getty Images

leader Joseph Stalin's collectivization of agriculture. By 1936 the Gulag held a total of 5,000,000 prisoners, a number that was probably equaled or exceeded every subsequent year until Stalin died in 1953. Besides rich or resistant peasants arrested during collectivization, persons sent to the Gulag included purged Communist Party members and military officers, German and other Axis prisoners of war (during World War II), members of ethnic groups suspected of disloyalty, Soviet soldiers and other citizens who had been taken prisoner or used as slave labourers by the Germans during the war, suspected saboteurs and traitors, dissident intellectuals, ordinary criminals, and many utterly innocent people who were hapless victims of Stalin's purges.

Inmates filled the Gulag in three major waves: in 1929–32, the years of the collectivization of Soviet agriculture; in 1936–38, at the height of Stalin's purges; and in the years immediately following World War II. Solzhenitsyn claimed

(continued on the next page)

that between 1928 and 1953 "some forty to fifty million people served long sentences in the Archipelago." Figures supposedly compiled by the Gulag administration itself (and released by Soviet historians in 1989) show that a total of 10 million people were sent to the camps in the period from 1934 to 1947. The true figures remain unknown.

At its height the Gulag consisted of many hundreds of camps, with the average camp holding 2,000–10,000 prisoners. Most of these camps were "corrective labour colonies" in which prisoners felled timber, laboured on general construction projects (such as the building of canals and railroads), or worked in mines. Most prisoners laboured under the threat of starvation or execution if they refused. It is estimated that the combination of very long working hours, harsh climatic and other working conditions, inadequate food, and summary executions killed off at least 10 percent of the Gulag's total prisoner population each year. Western scholarly estimates of the total number of deaths in the Gulag in the period from 1918 to 1956 range from 15 to 30 million.

The Gulag started to shrink soon after Stalin's death; hundreds of thousands of prisoners were amnestied from 1953 to 1957, by which time the camp system had returned to its proportions of the early 1920s. Indeed, the Gulag was officially disbanded; its activities were absorbed by various economic ministries, and the remaining camps were grouped in 1955 under a new body, GUITK (Glavnoye Upravleniye Ispravitelno-Trudovykh Kolony, or "Chief Administration of Corrective Labour Colonies").

crimes, the accused served as self-denounced scapegoats for catastrophes arising from the Secretary General's policies. Yet Stalin was successful in rapidly industrializing a backward country—as was widely acknowledged by enthusiastic contemporary foreign witnesses, including Adolf Hitler and such well-known writers as H.G. Wells and George Bernard Shaw.

While socialist ideology foresaw a "withering away" of the state as the classless society became a reality, Stalin asserted that the state must instead become stronger before it could be eliminated. Stalinism held that the enemies of socialism within and without Russia would try to avert the final victory of the Revolution. To face these efforts and protect the cause, it was argued, the state must be strong. Power became more and more centralized in Stalin, who in the late 1930s launched a bloody purge of all those he regarded as even potentially dangerous to the Soviet state. As part of the struggle against those whom he considered political rivals, Stalin identified political opposition with treason and used this as a weapon in his struggle against Leon Trotsky and Nikolay I. Bukharin and their supporters.

In late 1934—just when the worst excesses of Stalinism seemed to have spent themselves—the Secretary General launched a new campaign of political terror against the very Communist Party members who had brought him to power; his pretext was the assassination, in Leningrad on December 1, of his leading colleague and potential rival, Sergey Kirov. That Stalin himself had arranged Kirov's murder—as an excuse for the promotion of mass bloodshed—was strongly hinted by Nikita Khrushchev, first secretary of the party, in a speech denouncing Stalin at the 20th Party Congress in 1956.

Stalin used the show trial of leading Communists as a means for expanding the new terror. In August 1936, Grigory Zinoviev and Lev Kamenev were paraded in court to repeat fabricated confessions, sentenced to death, and shot; two more major trials followed, in January 1937 and March 1938. In June 1937, Marshal Mikhail Tukhachevsky, at the time the most influential military personality, and other leading generals were reported as court-martialed on charges of treason and executed.

Such were the main publicly acknowledged persecutions that empowered Stalin to tame the Soviet Communist Party and the Soviet elite as a whole. He not only "liquidated" veteran semi-independent Bolsheviks but also many party bosses, military leaders, industrial managers, and high government officials totally subservient to himself. Other victims included foreign Communists on Soviet territory and members of the very political police organization, now called the NKVD. All other sections of the Soviet elite—the arts, the academic world, the legal and diplomatic professions—also lost a high proportion of victims, as did the population at large, to a semi-haphazard, galloping persecution that fed on extorted denunciations and confessions. These implicated even more victims until Stalin himself reduced the terror, though he never abandoned it. His main motive was, presumably, to maximize his personal power.

By February 1939 most of the "Old Bolsheviks," those revolutionaries who in 1917 had begun the Revolution, had been exterminated. Millions more (estimated at from 7 million to 15 million) were sent to the forced-labour camps that Stalin made an integral part of the Soviet economy.

Three years after Stalin's death in 1953, Soviet leaders led by Nikita Khrushchev denounced the cult of Stalin and the terrorism perpetrated by his regime; they saw Stalinism as a temporary aberration in Soviet socialist development. Others saw it as a brutal but necessary and inevitable phase of that development. Still others saw in Stalinism an irrevocable Soviet break with the ideals of the Revolution.

In 1989 the Soviet historian Roy Medvedev estimated that about 20 million died as a result of the labour camps, forced collectivization, famine, and executions. Another 20 million were victims of imprisonment, exile, and forced relocation.

Fundamentalism

Fundamentalism is a type of militantly conservative religious movement characterized by the advocacy of strict conformity to sacred texts. Once used exclusively to refer to American Protestants who insisted on the inerrancy of the Bible, the term *fundamentalism* was applied more broadly beginning in the late 20th century to a wide variety of religious movements. Indeed, in the broad sense of the term, many of the major religions of the world may be said to have fundamentalist movements.

In the late 20th century the most influential—and the most controversial—study of fundamentalism was *The Fundamentalism Project* (1991–95), a series of five volumes edited by the American scholars Martin E. Marty and R. Scott Appleby. Marty and Appleby viewed fundamentalism primarily as the militant rejection of secular modernity. They argued that fundamentalism is not just traditional religiosity but an inherently political phenomenon, though this dimension may sometimes be dormant. Marty and Appleby also contended that fundamentalism is inherently totalitarian, insofar as it seeks to remake all aspects of society and government on religious principles.

Because the term *fundamentalism* is Christian in origin, because it carries negative connotations, and because its use in an Islamic context emphasizes the religious roots of the phenomenon while neglecting the nationalistic and social grievances that underlie it, many scholars prefer to call Islamic fundamentalists "Islamists" and to speak of "Islamist movements" instead of *Islamic fundamentalism*. (The members of these movements refer to themselves simply as Muslims.) Nevertheless, the term *Islamic fundamentalism* has been current in both popular and scholarly literature since the late 20th century.

The subject of Islamic fundamentalism attracted a great deal of attention in the West after the Iranian Revolution of 1978–79—which deposed Iran's ruler, Mohammad Reza Shah Pahlavi (1919–80), and established an Islamic republic—and especially after the September 11 attacks on the United States in 2001 by al-Qaeda, an international Islamist terrorist network. The spectacular nature of these events may have lent plausibility to the common but mistaken belief in the West that Islam and Islamic fundamentalism are closely connected, if not identical. In fact, however, not all Muslims believe that the Qur'ān is the literal and inerrant word of God, nor do all of them believe that Islam requires strict conformity to all the religious and moral precepts in the Qur'ān. More important, unlike genuine Islamic fundamentalists, most Muslims are not ideologically committed to the idea of a state and society based on Islamic religious law.

The character of Islamist movements varies greatly throughout the world. Some Islamists resort to terrorism, and some do not. Some espouse leftist political and economic programs, borrowing ideas from Marxism and other varieties of socialism, while others are more conservative. Most Islamists, however, insist on conformity to a code of conduct based on a literal interpretation of sacred scripture. They also insist that religion encompasses all aspects of life and hence that religion and politics cannot be separated. Like most fundamentalists, they generally have a Manichaean (dualistic) worldview: they believe that they are engaged in a holy war, or jihad, against their evil enemies, whom they often portray as pawns of Jewish and Masonic conspiracies in terms taken directly from the anti-Semitic literature of 20th-century Europe. Messianism, which plays an important role in Christian, Jewish, and Shīʿite Islamic fundamentalism, is less important in the fundamentalism of the Sunni branch of Islam.

The Ayatollah Ruhollah Khomeini during the Iranian Revolution. Michel
Setboun/Gamma-Rapho/Getty Images

Islamist movements have been politically signifi-cant in most Muslim countries primarily because they articulate political and social grievances better than do the established secular parties, some of which (the leftist parties) were discredited following the collapse of communism in Eastern Europe and the Soviet Union in 1990–91. Although the governments of Saudi Arabia and other oil-producing countries of the Persian Gulf region have represented them-selves as conforming strictly to Islamic law, they continue to face internal opposition from Islamist movements for their pro-Western political and economic policies, the extreme concentration of their countries' wealth in the hands of the ruling families, and, in the Islamists' view, the rulers' immoral lifestyles.

To some extent, the Islamists' hostility toward the West is symptomatic of the rejection of modernity attributed to all fundamentalist movements, since much of what is modern is derived from the West. (It should be noted, however, that Islamists do not reject modern technology.) But it would be a mistake to reduce all such hostility to a reactionary rejec-tion of all that is new; it would also be a mistake to attribute it entirely to xenophobia, though this is certainly an influ-ence. Another important factor is the Islamists' resentment of Western political and economic domination of the Middle East. This is well illustrated by the writings of Osama bin Laden, the founder and leader of al-Qaeda, which repeatedly condemn the United States for enabling the dispossession of the Palestinians, for orchestrating international sanctions on Iraq that contributed to the deaths of hundreds of thousands of Iraqi citizens in the 1990s, and for maintaining a military "occupation" of Saudi Arabia during the Persian Gulf War (1990–91). Bin Laden has also condemned the Saudi regime and most other governments of the Middle East for serving the interests of the United States rather than those of the

Islamic world. Thus, the fundamentalist dimension of bin Laden's worldview is interwoven with resentment of Western domination.

Puritanical revivalist movements calling for a return to the pristine Islam of the Prophet Muhammad have occurred periodically throughout Islamic history. During the period of European colonial rule in the 19th and 20th centuries, however, these movements began to take on a polemical, apologetic character. Muslim reformists such as Muḥammad 'Abduh (1849–1905) and Jamāl al-Dīn al-Afghānī (1838–97) stressed that a return to the "rationalist" Islam of Muhammad—which was not incompatible, in their view, with science and democracy—was essential if Muslims were to free themselves from European domination. This argument was subsequently adopted by some Islamic fundamentalists, though many others condemned democracy on the grounds that only God's laws are legitimate. Some Jewish and Christian fundamentalists have rejected democracy for the same reason.

Among the Islamist movements that have attracted the most attention in the West is the Palestinian movement Hamās, which was founded in 1987. Its name, which means "zeal" in Arabic, is an acronym of the name Ḥarakat al-Muqāwamah al-Islāmiyyah ("Islamic Resistance Movement"). Hamās was created primarily to resist what most Palestinians viewed as the occupation of their land by Israel. There is thus a clearly nationalist dimension to this movement, though it is also committed to the creation of a strictly Islamic state. Hamās opposed the idea of a Palestinian state in the West Bank and Gaza and insisted on fighting a jihad to expel the Israelis from all of Palestine—from the Jordan River to the Mediterranean and from Lebanon to Egypt. It justified its terrorist attacks on Israelis as legitimate acts of war against an occupying power. Like some other Islamist movements in the Middle East, Hamās provides basic social services—including schools, clinics, and food for the unemployed—that are not provided, or are inadequately provided, by local authorities. These charitable activities are an important source of its appeal among the Palestinian population.

In January 2006 Hamās was the victor by a wide margin in elections to the Palestinian Legislative Council, and it was asked to form a government. This development led to much speculation among political observers about whether Hāmas could evolve into a moderate nonviolent political party, as many other terrorist groups have done (e.g., Irgun Zvai Leumi and the Stern Gang in Israel and the Irish Republican Army in Ireland).

Although the terms *fundamentalism* and *fundamentalist* have entered common parlance and are now broadly applied, it should not be forgotten that the myriad movements so designated vary greatly in their origins, character, and outlook. Thus, Islamic fundamentalist movements differ from their Christian and Jewish counterparts in having begun as essentially defensive responses to European colonial domination. Early Islamic fundamentalists were reformers who wished to affirm the value of their religion by returning to what they sought to portray as its pristine original form; their movements only gradually acquired the militancy characteristic of much religious fundamentalism today. On the other hand, these movements share with Christian and Jewish fundamentalism an antipathy to secularism, an emphasis on the importance of traditional religiosity as their members understand it, and a strict adherence to sacred texts and the moral codes built upon them. Although these and other common features are important as sources of insight, each fundamentalist movement is in fact unique and is best understood when viewed in its own historical and cultural context.

CONCLUSION

A s we have seen, modern authoritarian forms of government have far-reaching roots in terms of historical precedent. In ancient Greece, tyrants rose to power to replace unpopular aristocratic regimes beginning around the 7th century BCE and largely oversaw the transition from those limited aristocracies to more democratic institutions. In the Roman Republic, the office of dictator took a different trajectory, progressing from a magistrate position temporarily granted extraordinary powers for the sake of handling internal crises to the infamous consulship of Julius Caesar, marked by the unchecked power he wielded. Throughout the latter half of the first millennium CE, various European rulers would come to employ the term *dictator* in times of revolution or social unrest, while *caudillismo*—in which a charismatic leader asserts power by force—dominated 19th-century Latin American politics.

It was the 20th century, nonetheless, that proved to be fertile soil for the development and implementation of modern autocratic governments. Defined by breaks in diplomacy, rivalries between major world powers, the emergence of new political systems to replace the classic European ones, and highly politicized economic relations between and within countries, the 20th century played witness to the rise of the totalitarian state as the chief alternative to constitutional democracies.

As totalitarian dictatorships developed in a variety of countries, it became clear that a complicated range of political systems—ones that many times, in principle, occupied opposing ends of the political spectrum—could play host to authoritarian governments. Fascism, an ideology that often nurtured totalitarian regimes, generally included right-wing, counterrevolutionary movements with highly militarized nationalistic goals helmed by charismatic leaders. This was the case of Nazi Germany under the self-styled *Führer* Adolf Hitler or Italy under the *duce*, Benito Mussolini.

In the Soviet Union and other communist states that sprouted throughout eastern Europe and developing nations after World War II, the principal political philosophy had an emphasis on the *international* nature of the workers revolution and the overthrow of capitalist society. Despite the fundamental differences between fascist ideology and left-wing communism, red leaders such as Joseph Stalin promoted single-party states whose official dogma, terroristic police forces, and state-controlled presses closely mirrored those that ruled by fascism.

Still yet, monocracy became a favoured form of government in the latter half of the 20th century in many postcolonial African and Asian states, as well as throughout much of Latin America as generals and military strongmen took power through coups d'état. Even Western constitutional democracies have resorted to increasing executive powers when faced with the extraordinary crises that the technological, industrialized era has brought on.

In each of its manifestations, authoritarianism has been used to preserve a sense of stability during turbulent times. Without judging the merits of the ideologies that these governments seek to protect, what can be said of all authoritarian movements is that they arise in response to a perceived national threat, be it internal or external. Under the battle cry of protecting valued institutions, the general populace is moved to temporarily forgo civil liberties or parliamentary democracy and grant an executive leader extreme power to keep stability. As the 21st century presents new challenges and technology changes the landscape of global politics, the question that remains unanswered is to what extent executive powers can be increased without drifting too far from the core principles of constitutional government.

GLOSSARY

absolutism The political doctrine and practice of unlimited, centralized authority and absolute sovereignty, as vested especially in a monarch or dictator.

authoritarianism Principle of blind submission to authority, as opposed to individual freedom of thought and action.

autocracy A form of government in which a country is ruled by a person or group with total power.

bossism The rule, practices, or system of a professional politician who controls a large number of votes in a party organization or who unofficially dictates appointments or legislative measures.

bourgeoisie In social and political theory, the social order dominated by the property-owning class.

commissar A Communist party official assigned to a military unit to teach party principles and policies and to ensure party loyalty.

communism Political theory advocating community ownership of all property, the benefits of which are to be shared by all according to the needs of each.

conscription The practice of ordering people by law to serve in the armed forces.

consulate The residence or official premises of a consul; capitalized, French government established after the Coup of 18–19 Brumaire (Nov. 9–10, 1799), during the French Revolution.

deist One who belongs to the movement or system of thought advocating natural religion, emphasizing morality, and in the 18th century denying the interference of the Creator with the laws of the universe.

demagogue A political leader who tries to get support by making false claims and promises and using arguments based on emotion rather than reason.

demonology A catalog of enemies or things that are viewed as viewed as evil or harmful.

fasces A bundle of rods and among them an ax with projecting blade borne before ancient Roman magistrates as a badge of authority.

graft The acquisition of gain (as money) in dishonest or questionable ways; also, illegal or unfair gain.

hoplite An ancient Greek heavily armed foot soldier whose function was to fight in close formation.

Manichaean A believer in religious or philosophical dualism.

monocratic Of or relating to government by a single person.

muzhik A Russian peasant.

nom de guerre Pseudonym.

phalanx In military science, tactical formation consisting of a block of heavily armed infantry standing shoulder to shoulder in files several ranks deep. Fully developed by the ancient Greeks, it survived in modified form into the gunpowder era and is viewed today as the beginning of European military development.

plebiscite A vote by which the people of an entire country or district express an opinion for or against a proposal especially on a choice of government or ruler.

pluralism In political science, the view that in liberal democracies power is (or should be) dispersed among a variety of economic and ideological pressure groups and is not (or should not be) held by a single elite or group of elites. Pluralism assumes that diversity is beneficial to society and that autonomy should be enjoyed by disparate functional or cultural groups within a society, including religious groups, trade unions, professional organizations, and ethnic minorities.

probity Adherence to the highest principles and ideals.

proletariat The labouring class; especially, the class of industrial workers who lack their own means of production and hence sell their labour to live.

statism The concentration of economic controls and planning in the hands of a highly centralized government often extending to government ownership of industry.

syndicalist Of or related to a movement that advocates direct action by the working class to abolish the capitalist order, including the state, and to establish in its place a social order based on workers organized in production units.

Teutonic Germanic.

tyrannicide The act of killing a tyrant.

BIBLIOGRAPHY

Fascism

General Studies

Stanley G. Payne, *A History of Fascism, 1914–1945* (1995), discusses fascist and extreme right movements in several countries, including the United States. Analyses of fascism in various European countries are presented in Alexander De Grand, *Fascist Italy and Nazi Germany* (1995); S.J. Woolf (ed.), *European Fascism* (1968); John Weiss, *The Fascist Tradition: Radical Right-Wing Extremism in Modern Europe* (1967); and Walter Laqueur and George L. Mosse (eds.), *International Fascism, 1920–1945* (1966). Arno J. Mayer, *Dynamics of Counterrevolution in Europe, 1870–1956: An Analytic Framework* (1971), is a study of collaboration and divergence between counterrevolutionaries and fascists. Alastair Hamilton, *The Appeal of Fascism: A Study of Intellectuals and Fascism, 1919–1945* (1971), discusses fascism in Italy, Germany, France, and Britain. On the social bases of European fascism, see Stein Ugelvik Larsen, Bertn Hagtvet, and Jan Petter Myklebust (eds.), *Who Were the Fascists: Social Roots of European Fascism* (1980); Detlef Mühlberger (ed.), *The Social Basis of European Fascist Movements* (1987); and Charles S. Maier, *Recasting Bourgeois Europe: Stabilization in France, Germany, and Italy in the Decade After World War I* (1975, reprinted 1988). Roger Griffen (ed.), *International Fascism* (1998), covers various theoretical approaches to fascism. Also of interest is Robert O. Paxton, "The Five Stages of Fascism," *Journal of Modern History*, 70(1) (March 1998), pp. 1–23; and Robert J. Soucy, "Functional Hating: French Fascist Demonology

Between the Wars," in *Contemporary French Civilization*, 23(2) (Summer/Fall 1999), pp. 158–176.

Italy

Basic works on Italian fascism include Alexander De Grand, *Italian Fascism: Its Origins & Development*, 3rd ed. (2000); Renzo De Felice, *Fascism: An Informal Introduction to Its Theory and Practice* (1977); and Edward R. Tannenbaum, *The Fascist Experience: Italian Society and Culture, 1922–1945* (1972). The experience of Jews and women is covered in Susan Zucotti, *The Italians and the Holocaust: Persecution, Rescue and Survival* (1987, reissued 1996); Victoria De Grazia, *How Fascism Ruled Women: Italy, 1922–1945* (1992); and Michael Ledeen, "Italian Jews and Fascism," *Judaism*, 18(3) (Summer 1969), pp. 277–298, respectively.

Germany

Analyses of the social bases of Nazism include Shelley Baranowski, *The Sanctity of Rural Life: Nobility, Protestantism, and Nazism in Weimar Prussia* (1995), and *The Confessing Church, Conservative Elites, and the Nazi State* (1986); Michael H. Kater, *The Nazi Party: A Social Profile of Members and Leaders, 1919–1945* (1983); and, on the Nazi Christian movement, Doris L. Bergen, *Twisted Cross: The German Christian Movement in the Third Reich* (1996). Intellectual and cultural precursors are covered in George L. Mosse, *Nazi Culture: Intellectual, Cultural, and Social Life in the Third Reich* (1966), and *The Crisis of German Ideology: Intellectual Origins of the Third Reich* (1964, reprinted 1981). Also of interest are Ian Kershaw, *Popular Opinion and Political Dissent in the Third Reich, Bavaria, 1933–1945* (1983); and David Schoenbaum, *Hitler's Social Revolution* (1966, reprinted 1980).

France, Russia, and Spain

Important studies of French fascism include Robert J. Soucy, *French Fascism: The Second Wave, 1933–1939* (1995), *French Fascism: The First Wave, 1924–1933* (1986), and *Fascist Intellectual: Drieu La Rochelle* (1979); Zeev Sternhell, *Neither Right nor Left: Fascist Ideology in France*, trans. by David Maisel (1986); and Eugen Joseph Weber, *Action Française: Royalism and Reaction in Twentieth Century France* (1962). Fascist movements in Russia and Spain are discussed in Walter Laqueur, *Black Hundred: The Rise of the Extreme Right in Russia* (1993); and Stanley G. Payne, *Falange: A History of Spanish Fascism* (1961).

Fascism outside Europe

Various non-European movements are covered in Stanley G. Payne, *A History of Fascism, 1914–1945*, cited above. Historical and contemporary studies of Argentine fascism are David Rock, *Authoritarian Argentina: The Nationalist Movement, Its History, and Its Impact* (1993); and Daniel James, *Resistance and Integration: Peronism and the Argentine Working Class, 1946–1976* (1988, reissued 1993). John Diggins, *Mussolini and Fascism: The View from America* (1972), discusses support for Italian fascism in the United States. Japanese fascism is covered in Masao Maruyama, *Thought and Behavior in Modern Japanese Politics*, expanded ed., edited by Ivan Morris (1969).

Neofascism

Richard Golsan, *Fascism's Return* (1998), is a broad survey. Neofascism in Italy, Germany, France, and Britain is discussed in Roger Eatwell, *Fascism: A History* (1995). Luciano Cheles, Ronnie Ferguson, and Michalina Vaughn (eds.), *The Far Right in Western and Eastern Europe* (1995), covers several neofascist movements. French neofascism is discussed in Jim Wolfreys, "Neither Right nor Left? Towards an Integrated Analysis of the Front National," in Nicholas Atakin and Frank Tallet (eds.), *The Right in France, 1789–1997* (1998). Russian neofascism is covered in Sven Gunnar Simonsen, *Politics and Personalities: Key Actors in the Russian Opposition* (1996); and Walter Laqueur, *Black Hundred: The Rise of the Extreme Right in Russia*, cited above. Jacques Julliard, *Ce fascisme qui vient* (1994), is a study of neofascism in the former Yugoslavia. Chilean neofascism is discussed in Mary Helen Spooner, *Soldiers in a Narrow Land: The Pinochet Regime in Chile* (1994).

Joseph Stalin

The standard Soviet edition of Stalin's works in Russian is Joseph Stalin, *Sochineniia*, 13 vol. (1946–51), covering publications up to January 1934. His later works have been issued in Russian in similar format by the Hoover Institution; Robert H. McNeal (ed.), *Sochineniia*, 3 vol. (1967), is considered to be the extension, as vol. 14–16, of the standard edition. The standard edition has been translated into English and published in Moscow: *Works*, 13 vol. (1952, reprinted 1975). A selection of Stalin's works in English is Bruce Franklin (ed.), *The Essential Stalin: Major Theoretical Writings, 1905–52* (1972). An annotated bibliography, Robert H. McNeal (compiler), *Stalin's Works* (1967), considers the authenticity of material in Russian attributed to Stalin.

There is no definitive biography of Stalin. The most useful of published studies include Dmitri Volkogonov, *Stalin: Triumph and Tragedy* (1991; originally published in Russian, 1989), based on archival sources; Robert Payne, *Rise and Fall of Stalin* (1965); Leon Trotsky, *Stalin: An Appraisal of the Man and His Influence, trans. from Russian*, new ed. (1967), and *The*

Stalin School of Falsification, 3rd ed. (1972; originally published in Russian, 1932), both denunciatory; Boris Souvarine, *Stalin: A Critical Survey of Bolshevism* (1939, reissued 1972; originally published in French, 1935); and Bertram D. Wolfe, *Three Who Made a Revolution*, 4th rev. ed. (1964, reissued 1984). T.H. Rigby (ed.), *Stalin* (1966), is an excellent short anthology of biographical and critical material. Other studies include Adam B. Ulam, *Stalin: The Man and His Era* (1973, reprinted 1987); Ronald Hingley, *Joseph Stalin: Man and Legend* (1974); Ian Grey, *Stalin: Man of History* (1979); Robert H. McNeal, *Stalin: Man and Ruler* (1988); Robert Conquest, *Stalin: Breaker of Nations* (1991); and Alan Bullock, *Hitler and Stalin: Parallel Lives* (1991).

Reliable, detailed firsthand accounts of Stalin's domestic background are few, the only family memoirs not subject to Stalinist censorship being those published after emigration by Stalin's daughter, Svetlana Alliluyeva, *Twenty Letters to a Friend* (1967; originally published in Russian in the United States, 1967), and *Only One Year* (1969; originally published in Russian in the United States, 1969). Soviet-censored memoirs by other family members are found in David Tutaev (trans. and ed.), *The Alliluyev Memoirs* (1968).

Studies of Stalin's prerevolutionary career include Edward Ellis Smith, *The Young Stalin: The Early Years of an Elusive Revolutionary* (1967), an attempt to prove that the subject was an agent of the tsarist political police; L. Beria, *On the History of the Bolshevik Organizations in Transcaucasia* (1949; originally published in Russian, 7th ed., 1947), the chief classic of Stalinist legend-building; and, on the historical context, Catherine Merridale, *Moscow Politics and the Rise of Stalin: The Communist Party in the Capital, 1925–32* (1990); Graeme Gill, *The Origins of the Stalinist Political System* (1990); Robert V. Daniels, *Trotsky, Stalin, and Socialism* (1991); and Robert C. Tucker, *Stalin as Rev-*

olutionary, 1879–1929: A Study in History and Personality (1973), and a sequel, *Stalin in Power: The Revolution from Above, 1928–1941* (1990).

Leonard Schapiro, *The Communist Party of the Soviet Union*, 2nd ed. (1970), is valuable on the political background of Stalin's mature career; as is John A. Armstrong, *The Politics of Totalitarianism* (1961). A more subjective version is Abdura-khman Avtorkhanov, *Stalin and the Soviet Communist Party: A Study in the Technology of Power* (1959; originally published in Russian in West Germany, 1959). Boris I. Nicolaevsky, *Power and the Soviet Elite* (1965, reissued 1975), is a collection of essays bearing on Stalin's activities from 1934 onward. Also of interest are Kendall E. Bailes, *Technology and Society Under Lenin and Stalin: Origins of the Soviet Technical Intelligentsia, 1917–1941* (1978); Eugène Zaleski, *Stalinist Planning for Economic Growth, 1933–1953* (1980; originally published in French, 1962); and Hiroaki Kuromiya, *Stalin's Industrial Revolution: Politics and Workers, 1928–1932* (1988).

Robert Conquest, *The Great Terror: Stalin's Purge of the Thirties*, rev. ed. (1973), is the fullest account of the massacres of 1937–38. Further studies are *The Great Purge Trial*, ed. by Robert C. Tucker and Stephen F. Cohen (1965), based on the official Soviet translation of the report of court proceedings; Joel Carmichael, *Stalin's Masterpiece: The Show Trials and Purges of the Thirties—The Consolidation of the Bolshevik Dictatorship* (1976); and Anton Antonov-Ovseyenko, *The Time of Stalin: Portrait of a Tyranny* (1981; originally published in Russian in the United States, 1980). F. Beck and W. Godin, *Russian Purge and the Extraction of Confession* (1951, trans. from German), remains a classic account of Stalin's reign of terror. W.G. Krivitsky, *In Stalin's Secret Service* (1939, reissued 1985; also published as *I was Stalin's Agent*, 1939, reissued 1992), is a firsthand account. Alexander Orlov, *The Secret History of Stalin's Crimes* (1953), contains informative primary sources. Nikolai Tolstoy, *Stalin's Secret War* (1981); and Adam Hochschild, *The Unquiet Ghost: Russians Remember Stalin* (1994), present testimony of victims of Stalin's purges.

On Stalin's role as wartime leader, an anthology of Soviet memoir material, Seweryn Bialer (ed.), *Stalin and His Generals* (1969, reprinted 1984), is useful; so, too, are Herbert Feis, *Churchill, Roosevelt, Stalin: The War They Waged and the Peace They Sought*, 2nd ed. (1967); Alexander Werth, *Russia at War, 1941–1945* (1964, reissued 1984); G.K. Zhukov, *Reminiscences and Reflections* (1969, reissued 1985; also published as *The Memoirs of Marshal Zhukov*, 1971; originally published in Russian, 1969); Albert Seaton, *Stalin as Military Commander* (1975; also published as *Stalin as Warlord*, 1976), based on the memoirs of Russian generals from 1918 to 1953; H. Montgomery Hyde, *Stalin: The History of a Dictator* (1971, reprinted 1982), especially useful for the coverage of World War II; John Erickson, *The Road to Stalingrad: Stalin's War with Germany* (1975, reprinted 1984), and *The Road to Berlin: Continuing the History of Stalin's War with Germany* (1983); Robin Edmonds, *The Big Three: Churchill, Roosevelt, and Stalin in Peace & War* (1991); and Amos Perlmutter, *FDR & Stalin: A Not So Grand Alliance, 1943–1945* (1993).

The postwar period is examined by William O. McCagg, *Stalin Embattled, 1943–1948* (1978), emphasizing foreign policy; Timothy Dunmore, *The Stalinist Command Economy: The Soviet State Apparatus and Economic Policy, 1945–53* (1980); William Taubman, *Stalin's American Policy: From Entente to Détente to Cold War* (1982); and Sergei N. Goncharov, John W. Lewis, and Xue Litai, *Uncertain Partners: Stalin, Mao, and the Korean War* (1993). Stalin's image after his death is explored in Columbia University, Russian Institute, *The Anti-Stalin Campaign and International Communism: A Selection of Documents*, rev. ed. (1956); Bertram D. Wolfe, *Khrushchev and Stalin's Ghost:*

Text, Background, and Meaning of Khrushchev's Secret Report to the Twentieth Congress on the Night of February 24–25, 1956 (1957, reprinted 1983); and T.H. Rigby, *The Stalin Dictatorship: Khrushchev's "Secret Speech" and Other Documents* (1968).

Stalin's influence on the arts is examined in Boris Groys (Boris Grois), *The Total Art of Stalinism: Avant-Garde, Aesthetic Dictatorship, and Beyond* (1992; originally published in German, 1988); Matthew Cullerne Bown, *Art Under Stalin* (1991); A. Kemp-Welch, *Stalin and the Literary Intelligentsia, 1928–39* (1991); and Frank J. Miller, *Folklore for Stalin: Russian Folklore and Pseudo-folklore of the Stalin Era* (1990). Studies of the effects of Stalinism on the 20th-century Communist movement include Alec Nove, *Stalinism and After*, 3rd ed. (1989); Roy A. Medvedev, *Let History Judge: The Origins and Consequences of Stalinism*, trans. from Russian, rev. and expanded ed. (1989), and *On Stalin and Stalinism*, trans. from Russian (1979); Robert C. Tucker (ed.), *Stalinism: Essays in Historical Interpretation* (1977); Robert C. Tucker, *The Soviet Political Mind: Stalinism and Post-Stalin Change*, rev. ed. (1971); Alan Wood, *Stalin and Stalinism* (1990); and Alec Nove (ed.), *The Stalin Phenomenon* (1993).

INDEX

Mexico, 18, 19, 67
Venezuela, 19
leadership principle, fascism and, 46–47
Le Bon, Gustave, 77, 79
Lenin, Vladimir, 58, 101, 124, 125, 136–138, 139, 140, 141
Leninism, 123, 124, 125, 136–138
Le Pen, Jean-Marie, 95–100
liberalism, fascist opposition to, 37–38

M

Maistre, Joseph de, 76, 77–78, 79
Mao Zedong/Maoism, 120–121, 124
Marty, Martin E., 147
Marx, Karl, 123–124, 136, 138
Marxism, 32–37, 40, 47, 48, 53, 54, 64, 68, 69, 73, 85, 123–124, 136–138, 148
Mauryan Empire, 119–120
Mexico, 18, 19, 67
military values, fascism and, 43
Milošević, Slobodan, 106–112
mobilization, fascism and, 44–46
Mukden Incident, 67
Mussolini, Benito, 26, 27, 29–31, 32, 34, 36, 38, 40, 42, 43, 46, 52, 53, 60, 62, 68, 72, 74–75, 76, 81, 82, 87, 89, 99, 114, 118, 154

N

Napoleon Bonaparte, 13–17
nationalism
    explanation and history of, 55–58
    fascism and, 53–54
National Socialism, 126–136
Nazism/Nazi Party, 20, 24, 29, 32, 34, 35, 38, 40, 41, 42, 44, 47, 50, 53, 54, 58–59, 60, 61, 62, 68–69,
72, 73–74, 80, 81, 82, 89, 90, 91, 93, 106, 111, 118, 122, 127, 130–136, 154
neofascism
    in Austria, 91–95
    in Croatia, 112–114
    definition of, 85
    in France, 95–100
    in Germany, 89–91
    in Italy, 87–89
    in Russia, 100–105
    in Serbia, 105–112
"new man," fascism and the, 47–48
Nietzsche, Friedrich, 77, 80, 126

O

Orthagoras, 2

P

Páez, José Antonio, 19
Paraga, Dobroslav, 112–114
Peisistratus, 2
Periander, 2
Perón, Isabel, 23, 115
Perón, Juan, 18, 19, 20–23, 114–115
personalismo, 18–19
Piłsudski, Józef, 26, 64
Pius XI, Pope, 74
Poland, 26, 39, 42, 57, 58, 62–64, 70, 72, 74, 81, 120, 135
populism, fascism and, 58–59
Primo de Rivera, José Antonio, 36, 50, 51, 62, 64–65

Q

Qaddafi, Muammar al–, 115

R

racism, fascism and, 68–72
Reign of Terror, 7–13
religious fundamentalism, 125, 147–152

revolutionary image, fascism and, 59–60

Robespierre, Maximilien de, 9–13

Russia, neofascism in, 100–105

S

Salazar, António de Oliveira, 26, 41, 46, 62, 76

Santa Anna, Antonio López de, 18, 19

scapegoating, fascism and, 54–58

Serbia, neofascism in, 105–112

sexism and misogyny, fascism and, 60–61

Solzhenitsyn, Aleksandr, 142, 143

South Africa, 27, 28, 66, 70, 85, 114, 115

Soviet Union, 24–25, 35, 58, 100, 103, 118, 120–121, 122, 123, 124, 125, 128, 135, 136–146, 150, 154

Spain, 18, 22, 34, 36, 43, 44, 50, 54, 57, 62, 64–65, 72, 73, 76, 78, 81, 82, 86, 99, 115

spirituality, fascism and, 51

SS, 48, 90, 91, 93, 132–134

Stalin, Joseph, 24, 58, 101, 118, 120, 122, 123, 125, 138–146, 154

Stalinism, 138–146

Sulla, Lucius Cornelius, 5, 6, 7

T

Taine, Hippolyte, 77, 79

Thrasybulus, 2

totalitarian ambitions, fascism and, 38–39

totalitarianism, definition of, 118

U

United States, 21, 26, 27, 44, 53, 55, 57, 66, 68, 70, 76, 98, 103, 104, 111, 117, 140, 147, 148, 150

V

Vasiliev, Dmitry, 101

Venezuela, 19

Versailles, Treaty of, 127–128

violence, fascism and, 51–53

Volksgemeinschaft, 28, 43–44

W

Weiss, John, 80, 82

World War I, 31, 32, 34, 35, 40, 57, 127–128, 135

World War II, 22, 23, 24, 26, 28, 31, 44, 48, 58, 73, 76, 85, 91, 97, 100, 111, 112, 114, 118, 120, 130, 131, 134, 135, 140, 143, 154

Y

youth glorification, fascism and, 48–50

Z

Zhirinovsky, Vladimir, 101–103